Implementing and Managing Microsoft® Exchange Server 2003 (70-284)

Lab Manual

Orin Thomas

PUBLISHED BY
Microsoft Press
A Division of Microsoft Corporation
One Microsoft Way
Redmond, Washington 98052-6399

Printed and bound in the United States of America.

4 5 6 7 8 9   QWT   9 8 7

Distributed in Canada by H.B. Fenn and Company Ltd.

A CIP catalogue record for this book is available from the British Library.

Microsoft Press books are available through booksellers and distributors worldwide. For further information about international editions, contact your local Microsoft Corporation office or contact Microsoft Press International directly at fax (425) 936-7329. Visit our Web site at www.microsoft.com/learning/. Send comments to *moac@microsoft.com*.

Project Editor: Barbara Moreland
Technical Editor: Elizabeth Cohn
Production: nSight, Inc.

SubAssy Part No. X1-04615
Body Part No. X11-04616

CONTENTS

LAB 1:   Active Directory Installation 1

Scenario. 1

Before You Begin 2

Exercise 1.1: Preparing the Server DNS Settings 2

Exercise 1.2: Installing Active Directory Using the Active
Directory Installation Wizard 4

Exercise 1.3: Creating a Child Domain in an Existing Forest. 7

Exercise 1.4: Installing Windows Server 2003 Support Tools. 9

Exercise 1.5: Configuring a Domain Controller as a Global
Catalog Server 10

Exercise 1.6: Raising the Domain Functional Level. 11

Review Questions. 13

Lab Challenge 1.1: Raising the Functional Level of the Forest to
Windows Server 2003 13

Lab Challenge 1.2: Changing Replication Schedule Using Active
Directory Sites and Services 14

LAB 2:   Installing Exchange Server 2003. 15

Scenario. 15

Before You Begin 16

Exercise 2.1: Preparing User Accounts for Installation. 16

Exercise 2.2: Running the Exchange Server Deployment Tools 19

Exercise 2.3: Installing Windows Server 2003 Components
Required to Support Exchange Server 2003 20

Exercise 2.4: Running ForestPrep in the Child Domain 21

Exercise 2.5: Configuring a Windows Server 2003 Forest With
ForestPrep. 23

Exercise 2.6: Configuring Windows Server 2003 Domains With
DomainPrep 24

Exercise 2.7: Installing Exchange Server 2003 in a New Exchange
Organization. 25

Exercise 2.8: Installing Exchange Server 2003 in an Existing
Exchange Organization. 26

Review Questions. 27

Lab Challenge 2.1: Identifying the New Groups and New User
Properties Created by DomainPrep 28

Lab Challenge 2.2: Identifying New Services Installed With
Exchange Server 2003. 28

LAB 3:   **Configuring a Microsoft Exchange Server 2003 Infrastructure**................**29**

Scenario... 29

Before You Begin 30

Exercise 3.1: Preparing Groups for the Delegation of Administrative Roles 30

Exercise 3.2: Exploring the Basic Functionality of Exchange System Manager..............................32

Exercise 3.3: The Delegation of Control Wizard 34

Exercise 3.4: Exploring Administrative Roles....................35

Exercise 3.5: Adding and Removing Exchange Server 2003 Components 37

Review Questions....................................38

Lab Challenge 3.1: Configuring New Administrative and Routing Groups and Switching from Mixed Mode to Native Mode...........39

LAB 4:   **Installing Microsoft Exchange Server 2003 Clusters and Front-End and Back-End Servers ...41**

Scenario... 41

Before You Begin 42

Exercise 4.1: Creating a Network Load Balancing Cluster........... 42

Exercise 4.2: Adding a Host to a Network Load Balancing Cluster 45

Exercise 4.3: Verifying a Network Load Balancing Cluster 46

Exercise 4.4: Removing a Network Load Balancing Cluster 49

Exercise 4.5: Configuring a Back-End Server......................50

Exercise 4.6: Configuring a Front-End Server 51

Exercise 4.7: Verifying Front-End Server Configuration..............53

Review Questions....................................53

Lab Challenge 4.1: Restoring to Previous Configuration 54

LAB A: **Troubleshooting Administrative Delegation and Exchange Configuration** **55**

Break Scenario 1....................................56

Break Scenario 2....................................57

LAB 5:   **Managing Recipient Objects and Address Lists ..59**

Scenario... 59

Before You Begin 60

Exercise 5.1: Creating and Initializing User Mailboxes..............61

Exercise 5.2: Mail-Enabling Contacts 63

Exercise 5.3: Creating a Mail-Enabled Distribution Group 64

Exercise 5.4: Deleting and Reconnecting Mailboxes 66

Exercise 5.5: Configuring Storage Limits on Individual Mailboxes 68

Exercise 5.6: Creating a Query-Based Distribution Group 69

Exercise 5.7: Creating a New Storage Group and Mailbox Store......70

Exercise 5.8: Moving a Storage Group............................71

Exercise 5.9: Creating an Offline Address List....................72

Exercise 5.10: Creating a New Recipient Policy....................73

Review Questions...75

Lab Challenge 5.1: Moving a Database Store.....................75

Lab Challenge 5.2: Changing a Mail Retention Policy..............76

LAB 6:   **Public Folders** **77**

Scenario..77

Before You Begin 78

Exercise 6.1: Preparation Tasks 78

Exercise 6.2: Creating Public Folders Using Outlook Web Access.....79

Exercise 6.3: Creating Public Folders Using Exchange
System Manager...81

Exercise 6.4: Creating a General-Purpose Public Folder Tree
and an Associated Store 82

Exercise 6.5: Mail-Enabling a Public Folder......................84

Exercise 6.6: Enabling the Security Tab On All Exchange
Server Objects...85

Exercise 6.7: Granting and Verifying Permissions to Create a
Top-Level Folder...86

Exercise 6.8: Configuring and Verifying Permissions to Access
Public Folders...87

Exercise 6.9: Replicating Public Folders.........................89

Review Questions...90

Lab Challenge 6.1: Creating a Public Store Policy 91

Lab Challenge 6.2: Modifying a Public Store Policy...............92

LAB 7:   **Virtual Servers**.............................**93**

Scenario... 93

Before You Begin 94

Exercise 7.1: Starting and Verifying the Default POP3 Virtual Server ..95

Exercise 7.2: Starting and Verifying the Default IMAP4 Virtual Server ..96

Exercise 7.3: Installing an Enterprise Root Certificate Authority 98

Exercise 7.4: Configuring SSL-Only Connections for the POP3
Virtual Server 101

Exercise 7.5: Configuring SSL Only Connections for the IMAP4
Virtual Server 103

Review Questions... 104

Lab Challenge 7.1: Configuring SSL Connections to Outlook
Web Access and Resolving Certificate Issues.................... 105

LAB 8:   SMTP Protocol Configuration and Management 107

Scenario 107

Before You Begin 108

Exercise 8.1: Configuring DNS to Support SMTP 108

Exercise 8.2: Configuring the SMTP Server to Require Authentication 110

Exercise 8.3: Configuring the Default SMTP Virtual Server to Only Accept SSL Connections 111

Exercise 8.4: Configuring Default SMTP Virtual Server Properties .. 113

Exercise 8.5: Creating and Configuring an SMTP Connector 115

Review Questions 116

Lab Challenge 8.1: Reconfiguring SMTP Settings for IMAP4 Accounts 116

Lab Challenge 8.2: Creating an Additional Virtual SMTP Server 117

LAB 9:   Microsoft Exchange Server 2003 Security 119

Scenario 119

Before You Begin 120

Exercise 9.1: Installing Exchange Server 2003 Service Pack 1 121

Exercise 9.2: Enabling Connection Filtering 122

Exercise 9.3: Blocking all E-Mail from a Specific E-Mail Address and an Entire Domain 123

Exercise 9.4: Creating a New Encryption and Digital Signature Certificate Template for Use by Exchange Users 125

Exercise 9.5: Using Digital Signatures and Encryption 126

Review Questions 128

Lab Challenge 9.1: Blocking Specific Domains from Sending SMTP Traffic to the Default SMTP Virtual Server 129

Lab Challenge 9.2: Creating an Advanced Exchange User Certificate Template 129

LAB B: Secure POP3 Access and Mailbox Problems 131

Break Scenario 1 131

Break Scenario 2 132

LAB 10:   Backup and Restore 133

Scenario 133

Before You Begin 134

Exercise 10.1: Creating a Recovery Storage Group 134

Exercise 10.2: Enabling the Volume Shadow Copy Service 136

Exercise 10.3: Performing a Full Online Backup of a Storage Group .. 137

Exercise 10.4: Public Folder Indexes 139

Exercise 10.5: Recovering a Deleted User's Mailbox 141

Exercise 10.6: Recovering a Mailbox Store Using the Recovery Storage Group 144

Exercise 10.7: Merging Recovered Mailbox Data 145

Review Questions 147

Lab Challenge 10.1: Volume Shadow Copies and Restoring the Executive SG 147

LAB 11:   **Monitoring Micorosoft Exchange Server 2003 . . 149**

Scenario 149

Before You Begin 150

Exercise 11.1: Filtering Exchange Events in the Application Log 150

Exercise 11.2: Monitoring Connected Users 152

Exercise 11.3: Monitoring User Mailbox Size 153

Exercise 11.4: Configuring Diagnostic Logging 153

Exercise 11.5: Specifying Events to Monitor 155

Exercise 11.6: Configuring Performance Counters 157

Exercise 11.7: Manually Defragmenting a Mailbox Store 160

Review Questions 161

Lab Challenge 11.1: Logging and Diagnostics 162

LAB 12:   **Troubleshooting Microsoft Exchange Server 2003 . . . . 163**

Scenario 163

Before You Begin 164

Exercise 12.1: Using Netdiag to Test Network Connectivity 164

Exercise 12.2: Using Dcdiag to Test Domain Controller Connectivity 165

Exercise 12.3: Verifying Mailbox Store Integrity 166

Exercise 12.4: Configuring a Queue Alert 167

Exercise 12.5: Using Telnet to Test the SMTP Server 169

Review Questions 171

Lab Challenge 12.1: Verifying the Integrity of the Executive Mailbox Store 171

Lab Challenge 12.2: Configuring an Alert for IMAP4 Authentication Failures 171

LAB C: **Restoring from Backup and Protocol Problems . . 173**

Break Scenario 1 173

Break Scenario 2 174

LAB 1
ACTIVE DIRECTORY INSTALLATION

This lab contains the following exercises and activities:

- Exercise 1.1: Preparing the Server DNS Settings

- Exercise 1.2: Installing Active Directory Using the Active Directory Installation Wizard

- Exercise 1.3: Creating a Child Domain in an Existing Forest

- Exercise 1.4: Installing Windows Server 2003 Support Tools

- Exercise 1.5: Configuring a Domain Controller as a Global Catalog Server

- Exercise 1.6: Raising the Domain Functional Level

- Review Questions

- Lab Challenge 1.1: Raising the Functional Level of the Forest to Windows Server 2003

- Lab Challenge 1.2: Changing Replication Schedule Using Active Directory Sites and Services

SCENARIO

Contoso, Ltd. is a large multinational company with branch offices located in the United States, the European Union, and Australia. Contoso has an aging network and mail infrastructure that management has decided to replace. After examining competing products, the company has decided that Microsoft Exchange Server 2003 best meets the business needs of Contoso. It has also decided that the best platform on which to run Exchange Server 2003 is Microsoft Windows Server 2003.

As senior systems administrator at Contoso, it has fallen to you to implement an Exchange Server 2003 and Windows Server 2003 pilot program. The pilot program will enable you to explore the details of implementing the features of these products without jeopardizing the day-to-day operation of Contoso's existing network infrastructure.

After completing this lab, you will be able to:

- Upgrade a stand-alone Windows Server 2003 computer to a domain controller using the Active Directory Installation Wizard.
- Create a new domain in an existing Windows Server 2003 forest.
- Convert a Windows Server 2003 computer to a global catalog server.
- Raise the functional level of a Windows Server 2003 domain.
- Raise the functional level of a Windows Server 2003 forest.

Estimated lesson time: 105 minutes

BEFORE YOU BEGIN

To successfully complete this lab, you will need the following:

- Two networked computers with Windows Server 2003 installed using stand-alone configuration
- Windows Server 2003 CD

> **IMPORTANT**   This lab is written to be performed on two computers. If each student has only a single computer, students can work as partners and share computers when needed. The first computer will be Computerxx, and the second computer will be Computeryy. Computerxx typically has an odd-numbered name, such as Computer01 and Computer03. Computeryy typically has an even-numbered name, such as Computer02 and Computer04. If you are unsure of your computer's name, at a command prompt run the hostname command to find out what it is. Unless otherwise specified, all user accounts used in this lab use the password P@ssw0rd.

EXERCISE 1.1: PREPARING THE SERVER DNS SETTINGS

Estimated completion time: 10 minutes

Exchange Server 2003 and the Active Directory directory service are both highly dependent on the Domain Name System (DNS). When setting up a new domain, you need to configure a DNS server to host the name information for that domain. If you have not already configured a DNS server to host that information, the Active Directory installation process automatically installs the DNS service.

To simulate this for your pilot program, you will change the Transmission Control Protocol/Internet Protocol (TCP/IP) settings of the Windows Server 2003 computer that you wish to promote to domain controller so that it looks toward itself to resolve DNS requests.

IMPORTANT   *Complete the following tasks on Computerxx.*

1. Log on to Computerxx with the Administrator account. The password is P@ssw0rd or one assigned to you by your lab proctor.

2. Open a Command Prompt window, type **ipconfig**, and press ENTER. Note the IP address of the computer.

3. Click Start, point to Control Panel, point to Network Connections, right-click Local Area Connection, and then select Properties.

   The Local Area Connection Properties dialog box opens.

4. Select Internet Protocol (TCP/IP), and then click Properties.

   The Internet Protocol (TCP/IP) Properties dialog box opens.

5. In the Preferred DNS Server text box, type the IP address that you ascertained in step 2. (The IP address should be the same as the address in the IP Address box.) Figure 1-1 shows the settings for Computer03.

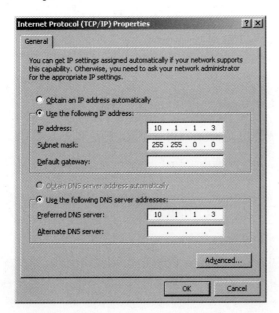

Figure 1-1   Setting the preferred DNS server

6. Click OK to accept your changes.

IMPORTANT   *Complete the following tasks on Computeryy.*

7. Repeat steps 1, 3, 4, 5, and 6 on Computer*yy*. Be sure to use the IP address of Computer*xx*, not Computer*yy*, for Computer*yy*'s Preferred DNS Server setting.

> **QUESTION**   What advanced options are available on the Advanced tab of the Local Area Connection Properties dialog box? What do they do?

8. Close all open windows on both computers.

EXERCISE 1.2: INSTALLING ACTIVE DIRECTORY USING THE ACTIVE DIRECTORY INSTALLATION WIZARD

Estimated completion time: 20 minutes

The first part of the pilot program at Contoso, Ltd. involves installing Active Directory on the first domain controller in the forest. The Active Directory Installation Wizard provides the most common way to install Active Directory on a Windows Server 2003 computer. Issuing the dcpromo command starts the Active Directory Installation Wizard.

To install Active Directory on a Windows Server 2003 stand-alone system and create a new domain in a new forest, complete the following steps.

> **IMPORTANT**   Complete the following tasks using Computer*xx*.

1. On Computer*xx*, click Start, and then click Run.

   The Run dialog box appears.

2. In the Open box, type **dcpromo.exe**, and then click OK.

   The Active Directory Installation Wizard launches.

3. On the Welcome To The Active Directory Installation Wizard page, click Next.

4. On the Operating System Compatibility page, click Next.

5. On the Domain Controller Type page, select Domain Controller For A New Domain, as shown in Figure 1-2. Click Next.

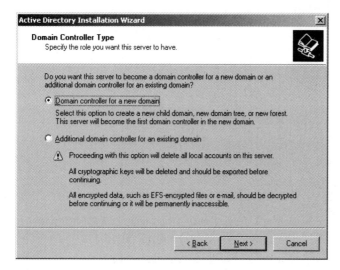

Figure 1-2 Selecting domain controller type

6. On the Create New Domain page, ensure that Domain In A New Forest is selected and then click Next.

7. On the New Domain Name page, type the name of your domain in the Full DNS Name For New Domain text box. Your domain is named **contosoxx.com** (where *xx* is the number of your computer). Click Next.

8. On the NetBIOS Domain Name page, the Active Directory Installation Wizard suggests a NetBIOS name (CONTOSO*xx*). Accept the default name provided by clicking Next.

> **QUESTION** What is the difference between a NetBIOS name and a full DNS name?

9. On the Database And Log Folders page, accept the defaults by clicking Next.

10. On the Shared System Volume page, leave the default location of the Sysvol folder in the Folder Location box. The Sysvol folder must reside on a partition or volume formatted with the NTFS file system. Click Next.

11. On the DNS Registration Diagnostics page, select Install And Configure The DNS Server On This Computer, and then click Next.

12. On the Permissions page, read through the available options as shown in Figure 1-3. It is best practice to accept the default option of Permissions Compatible Only With Windows 2000 Or Windows Server 2003 Operating Systems. Leave the default option selected, and then click Next.

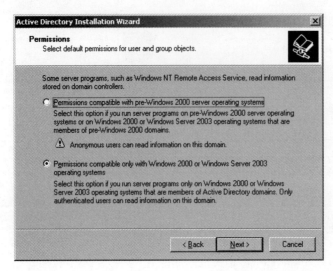

Figure 1-3   The Permissions page of the Active Directory Installation Wizard

13. On the Directory Services Restore Mode Administrator Password page, type the password **P@ssw0rd** in the Restore Mode Password text box. It is important to remember that the Directory Services Restore Mode Administrator Password is not necessarily the same as the Administrator password. Many administrators have failed to enter Directory Services Restore Mode because they enter the Administrator password rather than the separate Directory Services Restore Mode Administrator Password. Confirm the password in the Confirm Password box. Click Next.

14. The Summary page displays the options that you have selected through the wizard, as shown in Figure 1-4. Review the contents of this page for accuracy, and then click Next.

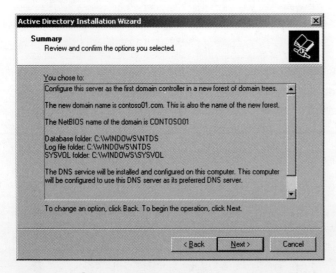

Figure 1-4   Summary page

The wizard takes a few minutes to configure Active Directory components. You might be prompted to insert your Windows Server 2003 CD.

15. When the Completing The Active Directory Installation Wizard page appears, click Finish, and then click Restart Now.

EXERCISE 1.3: CREATING A CHILD DOMAIN IN AN EXISTING FOREST

Estimated completion time: 20 minutes

Contoso eventually will implement a Windows Server 2003 forest containing several child domains. A different child domain will be used in each country where Contoso has a corporate presence. To simulate this in the lab, you will create a child domain of the contosoxx.com domain.

To configure a stand-alone Windows Server 2003 computer as a domain controller for a new domain in an existing forest, follow these steps.

> **IMPORTANT**   *Complete the following tasks using Computeryy.*

1. Log on to Computeryy with the Administrator account using the password P@ssw0rd.

2. On Computeryy, click Start, and then click Run. The Run dialog box appears.

3. In the Open box, type **dcpromo.exe**, and then click OK.

4. The Active Directory Installation Wizard launches. Click Next.

5. The Operating System Compatibility warning appears. Click Next.

6. On the Domain Controller Type page, select Domain Controller For A New Domain, as shown earlier in Figure 1-2. Click Next.

7. On the Create New Domain page, select Child Domain In An Existing Domain Tree, as shown in Figure 1-5. Click Next.

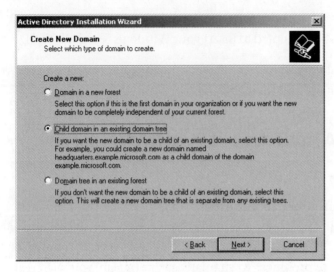

Figure 1-5   Creating a new domain tree in an existing forest

8. On the Network Credentials page enter the Administrator username and the password **P@ssw0rd**. Ensure that the domain is set to contoso*xx*.com. Click Next.

9. You will be asked to enter the full DNS name of the parent domain. You can use the Browse button to select contoso*xx*.com. You also will need to enter the child domain name. Enter contoso*yy* (where *yy* is the number of this computer). The Child Domain Installation page is shown in Figure 1-6. Click Next.

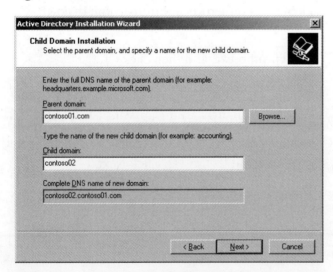

Figure 1-6   Create a new child domain

10. On the NetBIOS Domain Name page, the Active Directory Installation Wizard will suggest a NetBIOS name (CONTOSO*yy*). Accept the default name provided by clicking Next.

11. On the Database And Log Folders page, accept the defaults by clicking Next.

12. On the Shared System Volume page, leave the default location of the Sysvol folder in the Folder Location box. Click Next.

13. On the DNS Registration Diagnostics page, you should receive a note that DNS registration support for this domain controller has been verified. Click Next.

> **QUESTION**   Why do you not have to install a new DNS server for the child domain?

14. On the Permissions page, leave the default option selected, and then click Next

15. On the Directory Services Restore Mode Administrator Password page, type the password **P@ssw0rd** in the Restore Mode Password box and in the Password Confirmation box. Click Next.

16. The Summary page is displayed. It should be similar to Figure 1-4, but with a different domain name. Note that the summary also mentions that the new domain is a child domain of contoso*xx*.com. Click Next.

17. The wizard will take a few moments to configure Active Directory. You might be prompted to insert your Windows Server 2003 CD.

18. When the Completing The Active Directory Installation Wizard page appears, click Finish, and then click Restart Now.

EXERCISE 1.4: INSTALLING WINDOWS SERVER 2003 SUPPORT TOOLS

Estimated completion time: 10 minutes

The Windows Support Tools are a collection of utilities that can help you diagnose problems with your network infrastructure. The tools come in an edition for both Windows 2000 and Windows Server 2003 and are located on the installation media. After reading the Exchange Server 2003 setup documentation you determine that it would be useful to have the Windows Support Tools installed on each of the computers on which you will install Exchange Server 2003.

To install the Windows Server 2003 Support Tools, complete the following steps.

> **IMPORTANT**   Complete the following tasks using Computer*xx* and Computer*yy*.

1. Ensure that the Windows Server 2003 installation media is present

2. Using My Computer, navigate to the Support\Tools directory of the Windows Server 2003 installation media.

3. To install, double-click the file Suptools.msi. This launches the Windows Support Tools Setup Wizard. Click Next.

4. On the End User License Agreement page, select I Agree, and click Next.

5. On the User Information page, click Next.

6. On the Destination Directory page, leave the default values in place, and click Install Now. After several moments, when the installation has completed, click Finish to exit the wizard.

7. Verify that installation has completed successfully by confirming that the Windows Support Tools program group is present in the All Programs area of the Start menu.

EXERCISE 1.5: CONFIGURING A DOMAIN CONTROLLER AS A GLOBAL CATALOG SERVER

Estimated completion time: 10 minutes

Global catalog servers store partial replicas of Active Directory objects located in other domains in a forest. Placing a global catalog at each site when a geographically dispersed forest is used for an organization can significantly improve the performance of Exchange Server 2003 in locating objects such as address lists. The first domain controller in a forest is automatically configured as a global catalog server. Additional global catalog servers must be configured manually.

To install a global catalog server on a domain controller that is not configured as a global catalog server, complete the following steps.

IMPORTANT   *Complete the following tasks using Computeryy.*

1. On Computeryy, click Start, open the Administrative Tools folder, and then open Active Directory Sites And Services.

2. Expand the Computeryy node, and select the NTDS Settings as shown in Figure 1-7.

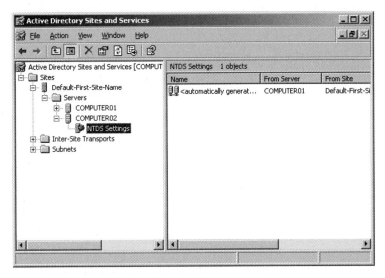

Figure 1-7   The NTDS settings of Computer*yy*

3. From the Action menu, select Properties. Select the Global Catalog check box as shown in Figure 1-8, and then click OK.

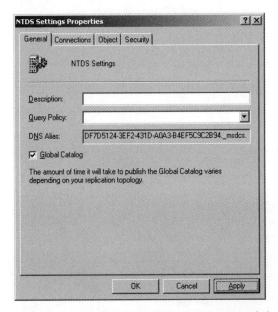

Figure 1-8   Configuring Computer*yy* as a global catalog server

4. Close the Active Directory Sites And Services window.

EXERCISE 1.6: RAISING THE DOMAIN FUNCTIONAL LEVEL

Estimated completion time: 15 minutes

Domain functional levels determine which operating systems can be used for domain controllers and which features of Windows Server 2003 are enabled. The lower the domain functional level, the fewer features are supported. In mixed environments where Microsoft Windows NT 4 and Windows 2000 domain controllers are still used to authenticate logons, a low domain functional level such as Windows 2000 Mixed might be necessary. As Contoso will be deploying Exchange Server 2003 only in domains where logons are authenticated against Windows Server 2003, part of the pilot program is to maximize the number of available features by raising the domain functional level to its highest possible setting.

To raise the functional level of a domain, complete the following steps.

> **IMPORTANT** Complete the following tasks using Computerxx and Computeryy.

1. Click Start, navigate to the Administrative Tools menu, and then select Active Directory Domains And Trusts.

2. If you are using Computerxx, click the contosoxx.com node and from the Action menu, select Raise Domain Functional Level. If you are using Computeryy, click the contosoyy.contosoxx.com node and from the Action menu, select Raise Domain Functional Level.

3. On the Raise Domain Functional Level page, use the drop-down list to select Windows Server 2003 as the functional level, as shown in Figure 1-9.

> **QUESTION** What are the different functional levels that you can have a Windows Server 2003 domain set to? (Hint: Check Help.)

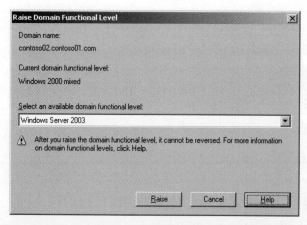

Figure 1-9   Raising the domain functional level

4. Once the correct functional level is selected, click Raise.

> **QUESTION** Why must you be completely certain that raising the domain functional level is the correct course of action?

5. Read the warning, and then click OK.

6. Once the functional level is raised successfully, click OK and close Active Directory Domains And Trusts.

REVIEW QUESTIONS

Estimated completion time: 20 minutes

1. In your own words, describe what you learned during this lab.

2. Why, in Exercise 1.2, were you asked to configure a domain in a new forest? Why not configure a domain within an existing forest?

3. In what cases would you select alternate permissions for step 12 of Exercise 1.2?

4. Why does the normal Administrator account password not always work in Directory Services Restore Mode?

5. Why does a domain controller hosting a DNS server require a static IP address?

LAB CHALLENGE 1.1: RAISING THE FUNCTIONAL LEVEL OF THE FOREST TO WINDOWS SERVER 2003

Estimated completion time: 15 minutes

Part of the pilot program involves assessing the knowledge that you have gained to this point. That includes performing small tasks that you don't have the full instructions for, but that you should be able to complete by using the knowledge you have gained during today's exercises. After reading more about Windows Server 2003 in your research for the pilot program, you have determined that you need to raise the functional level of your forest to Windows Server 2003. This will allow you to take full advantage of all of the new features of Windows Server 2003.

IMPORTANT Complete the following tasks on Computerxx.

■ Using the Active Directory Domains And Trusts console, raise the forest functional level to Windows Server 2003.

■ At the end of the process, provide a screen shot for your instructor that shows that the forest functional level is set to Windows Server 2003 and cannot be raised further. You can take a screen shot of the entire screen by pressing PRINTSCREEN, or you can take a screen shot of the active window by pressing ALT + PRINTSCREEN. Then open Microsoft Paint, and from the Edit menu, select Paste. Save the resulting picture for submission.

LAB CHALLENGE 1.2: CHANGING REPLICATION SCHEDULE USING ACTIVE DIRECTORY SITES AND SERVICES

Estimated completion time: 15 minutes

Part of the pilot program involves assessing the knowledge that you have gained to this point. That includes performing small tasks that you don't have the full instructions for, but that you should be able to complete by using the knowledge you have gained during today's exercises. Use the Active Directory Sites And Services console to change the replication schedule for Computerxx (or Computeryy) from one time per hour to four times per hour. Take a screenshot displaying the new schedule and save it for submission.

LAB 2
INSTALLING EXCHANGE SERVER 2003

This lab contains the following exercises and activities:

■ Exercise 2.1: Preparing User Accounts for Installation

■ Exercise 2.2: Running the Exchange Server Deployment Tools

■ Exercise 2.3: Installing Windows Server 2003 Components Required to Support Exchange Server 2003

■ Exercise 2.4: Running ForestPrep in the Child Domain

■ Exercise 2.5: Configuring a Windows Server 2003 Forest with ForestPrep

■ Exercise 2.6: Configuring Windows Server 2003 Domains with DomainPrep

■ Exercise 2.7: Installing Exchange Server 2003 in a New Exchange Organization

■ Exercise 2.8: Installing Exchange Server 2003 in an Existing Exchange Organization

■ Review Questions

■ Lab Challenge 2.1: Identifying the New Groups and New User Properties Created by DomainPrep

■ Lab Challenge 2.2: Identifying New Services Installed with Exchange Server 2003

SCENARIO

Now that you have created a Microsoft Windows Server 2003 forest of two domains to be used in the Contoso Microsoft Exchange Server 2003 pilot program, it is time to create the administrative accounts that you will use for the installation of Exchange Server 2003; run diagnostics on the pilot network infrastructure; prepare Windows Server 2003, the forest, and domain for the installation of Exchange Server 2003; and then finally install Exchange Server 2003 in both the root and child domains.

The goal of this aspect of the pilot program is to bring an understanding of the process involved in installing Exchange Server 2003 to your team. As Contoso is a huge multinational organization, it is impractical for you to personally visit each site and perform the installation yourself. Once your team understands the Exchange Server 2003 installation process, you will be able to confidently send them out to branch office locations to install Exchange Server 2003.

After completing this lab, you will be able to:
- Perform network and Active Directory diagnostics.
- Prepare Windows Server 2003 for the installation of Exchange Server 2003.
- Prepare a Windows Server 2003 forest using ForestPrep.
- Prepare a Windows Server 2003 domain using DomainPrep.
- Install Exchange Server 2003 Enterprise Edition.

Estimated lesson time: 105 minutes

BEFORE YOU BEGIN

To successfully complete this lab, you will need the following:

- Two networked computers with Windows Server 2003 installed using stand-alone configuration according to the setup guide

- Windows Server 2003 CD

- To have completed all exercises in Lab 1

> **IMPORTANT** This lab is written to be performed on two computers. If each student has only a single computer, students can work as partners and share computers when needed. The first computer will be Computerxx, and the second computer will be Computeryy. Computerxx typically has an odd-numbered name, such as Computer01 and Computer03. Computeryy typically has an even-numbered name, such as Computer02 and Computer04. If you are unsure of your computer's name, run a command prompt and run the hostname command to find out. Unless otherwise specified, all user accounts used in this lab use the password P@ssw0rd.

EXERCISE 2.1: PREPARING USER ACCOUNTS FOR INSTALLATION

Estimated completion time: 10 minutes
Rather than installing Exchange Server 2003 using the existing user accounts of members of your team, you have decided that it is better to create unique

accounts to be used for specific stages of Exchange Server 2003 installation. This helps with auditing and security. You can disable an account once it has performed its designated function. You can also check whether an account created for one purpose is being used for another. If such a case arises, it is a sure sign that security has in some way been compromised. It is more difficult to spot unusual activity if diverse administrative functions are performed using the same account.

IMPORTANT   *Complete the following tasks on Computerxx.*

1. Log on with the Administrator account.

2. From the Administrative Tools menu, open Active Directory Users And Computers.

3. Create the following user accounts in the user's container in the Contosoxx.com domain as shown in Figure 2-1.

    ❑ Exchange.forestprep

    ❑ Exchange.domainprep

    ❑ Exchange.fulladmin

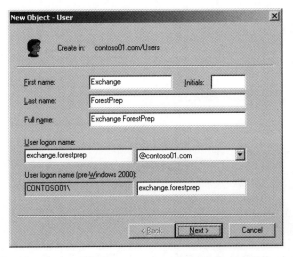

Figure 2-1   Creating a user account in Active Directory Users And Computers

Assign all accounts the password P@ssw0rd. Ensure that the user does not have to change the password at next logon and that the password never expires.

IMPORTANT   *Complete the following tasks on Computeryy.*

4. Log on with the Administrator account. The password is **P@ssw0rd** or one assigned to you by your lab proctor.

5. From the Administrative Tools menu, open Active Directory Users And Computers.

6. Create the following single user account in the Users container in the Contosoyy.Contosoxx.com domain.

   ❑ Exchange.domainprep

   Assign all accounts the password P@ssw0rd. Ensure that the user does not have to change the password at next logon and that the password never expires.

7. Add the accounts to the following groups as shown in Figure 2-2:

User	Contosoxx Groups	Contosoyy Groups
Contosoxx\Exchange.forestprep	Schema Admins, Enterprise Admins	Administrators
Contosoxx\Exchange.domainprep	Domain Admins	
Contosoyy\Exchange.domainprep		Domain Admins
Contosoxx\Exchange.fulladmin	Administrators	Administrators

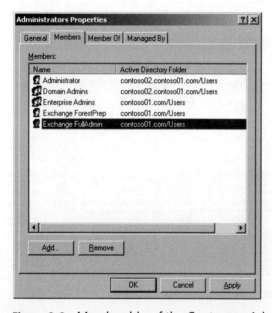

Figure 2-2   Membership of the Contosoyy Administrators group

> **QUESTION**   Why can't you add the Exchange.domainprep account from the Contosoyy domain to the Domain Admins group in the Contosoxx domain?

> **QUESTION**   What are the benefits of creating unique accounts for specific administrative tasks?

8. Close all open windows on both computers.

EXERCISE 2.2: RUNNING THE EXCHANGE SERVER DEPLOYMENT TOOLS

Estimated completion time: 10 minutes

Although you will not be using the Exchange Server 2003 Deployment Tools checklist directly during the pilot program at Contoso, you deem knowledge of it important enough that it is worth showing to your support team. This aspect of the pilot program itself was developed after reviewing the objectives. You hope that your team members will find the deployment tools of use when they are sent to remove Contoso sites to install Exchange Server 2003 during the organization's rollout.

> **IMPORTANT** Complete the following tasks using Computerxx and Computeryy.

1. Place the Exchange Server 2003 Enterprise Edition evaluation CD into the CD-ROM drive.

   The Exchange Server 2003 Enterprise Edition splash screen appears.

2. Click Exchange Deployment Tools. The Exchange Server Deployment Tools screen shown in Figure 2-3 appears.

Figure 2-3 The Exchange Server Deployment Tools screen

> **QUESTION** What does Microsoft recommend that you do prior to using the Exchange Server Deployment Tools?

3. Click Deploy The First Exchange 2003 Server.

4. Click New Exchange 2003 Installation.

5. Review the checklist presented on the Exchange Server Deployment Tools for a New Exchange 2003 Installation.

> **QUESTION** According to the checklist, which services need to be installed and enabled on Windows Server 2003 prior to performing a new Exchange 2003 installation?

6. Close the Exchange Server Deployment Tools and the Microsoft Exchange Server 2003 splash screen.

EXERCISE 2.3: INSTALLING WINDOWS SERVER 2003 COMPONENTS REQUIRED TO SUPPORT EXCHANGE SERVER 2003

Estimated completion time: 10 minutes

One aspect of Exchange Server 2003 that proved popular with management when Contoso was evaluating rival mail systems was Microsoft Outlook Web Access. To support Outlook Web Access, Windows Server 2003 must have the World Wide Web Publishing Service and ASP.NET installed and running. By default, Windows Server 2003 does not have these services installed. This makes Windows Server 2003 more secure out of the box, but also means that administrators must manually install and enable these services if they wish to utilize them.

> **IMPORTANT** Complete the following tasks using Computerxx and Computeryy.

1. Replace the Exchange Server 2003 Enterprise Edition evaluation CD with the Windows Server 2003 Enterprise Edition evaluation CD. Close the splash screen if it appears.

2. Open Add/Remove Programs in Control Panel.

3. Select the Add/Remove Windows Components option. Select Application Server, and click Details.

4. Select Internet Information Services (IIS), and click Details.

5. Select the Common Files, Internet Information Services Manager, NNTP Service, SMTP Service, and World Wide Web Service check boxes. Click OK.

6. Select the ASP.NET check box as shown in Figure 2-4.

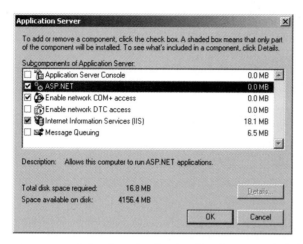

Figure 2-4 Selections in the Application Server dialog box

> **QUESTION** Why does Internet Information Services (IIS) appear with a grayed-out check box rather than a white check box like ASP.NET?

7. Click OK, and then click Next. The Configuring Components screen appears. If you did not place the Windows Server 2003 Enterprise Edition CD into your CD-ROM drive, you will be asked to do so or to specify an alternate location for the installation files.

8. When the installation finishes, open the Services console from Administrative Tools and verify that the NNTP, SMTP, and World Wide Web publishing services have started.

> **QUESTION** What is the startup type of these services, and which account do they log on as?

9. Log off from the computer.

EXERCISE 2.4: RUNNING FORESTPREP IN THE CHILD DOMAIN

Estimated completion time: 10 minutes

After looking at the documentation for the use of ForestPrep, you notice that you cannot run ForestPrep in the child domain. To reinforce this to your team, you wish to demonstrate to them what happens when you attempt to run ForestPrep in the child domain of a Windows Server 2003 forest.

> **IMPORTANT** Complete the following tasks using Computeryy.

1. Log on to Computeryy using the account Exchange.forestprep and the password P@ssw0rd. Ensure that you set the Log On To: drop-down list box to Contosoxx as shown in Figure 2-5.

Figure 2-5 Have the account validated by the correct domain

> **QUESTION** What would happen if you tried to log in without adding the Exchange.forestprep user account to the Contosoyy built-in Administrators group?

2. Place the Exchange Server 2003 Enterprise Edition CD into the computer's CD-ROM drive.

3. Open a command prompt. Navigate to D:\Setup\I386 (where D is the drive letter assigned to the CD-ROM drive).

4. Issue the setup /forestprep command.

5. Setup will start. On the Microsoft Exchange Installation Wizard page, click Next.

6. On the License Agreement page, review the license, select I Agree, and then click Next.

7. On the Component Selection page, in the Microsoft Exchange Component name drop-down list box, select ForestPrep.

8. Carefully review the error message that appears.

> **QUESTION** Under what conditions could you run ForestPrep in a child domain of a Windows Server 2003 forest?

9. Answer OK to the error message. Close all windows, and log off Computeryy.

EXERCISE 2.5: CONFIGURING A WINDOWS SERVER 2003 FOREST WITH FORESTPREP

Estimated completion time: 10 minutes

Rather than transfer the schema master to the child domain, you will run Forest-Prep in the root domain, Contoso*xx*. To run ForestPrep in the root domain:

> **IMPORTANT**   *Complete the following tasks using Computerxx.*

1. Ensure that the Exchange Server 2003 Enterprise Edition CD is in the computer's CD-ROM drive.

2. Log on to Computer*xx* using the Exchange.forestprep user account and the password P@ssw0rd.

3. Open a command prompt. Navigate to D:\Setup\I386 (where D is the drive letter assigned to the CD-ROM drive).

4. Issue the setup /forestprep command.

5. Setup will start. On the Microsoft Exchange Installation Wizard page, click Next.

6. On the License Agreement page, review the license, select I Agree, and then click Next.

> **NOTE**   *Note that unlike when you attempted to run ForestPrep in the child domain, there is no need to change any settings on the Component Selection page.*

7. On the Component Selection page, shown in Figure 2-6, click Next.

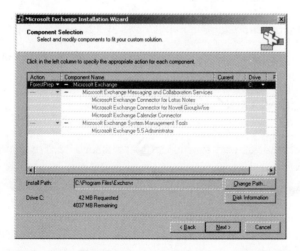

Figure 2-6   The Component Selection page for ForestPrep

8. On the Microsoft Exchange Server Administrator Account page, ensure that you change the default setting to contoso*xx*\exchange.fulladmin. Click Next.

9. The ForestPrep process begins.

> **QUESTION** *Why does ForestPrep need to be run in the same domain as the schema master?*

10. When the ForestPrep process finishes, log off Computer*xx*.

EXERCISE 2.6: CONFIGURING WINDOWS SERVER 2003 DOMAINS WITH DOMAINPREP

Estimated completion time: 10 minutes

Once the ForestPrep process has modified the forest schema, it is time to prepare the domains using the DomainPrep utility. DomainPrep should be used in those domains that will have mail-enabled users or objects. As all of the domains in the Contoso organization will eventually have mail-enabled users, your support team needs to become familiar with this process. Unlike ForestPrep, the administrative requirements for DomainPrep are only that the user be a member of the Domain Admins group for the domain in which DomainPrep is being run.

> **IMPORTANT** *Complete the following tasks using Computerxx and Computeryy.*

1. Log on to the computer using the relevant domain's Exchange.domainprep account with the password P@ssw0rd.

> **NOTE** *Remember that each domain has its own exchange.domainprep account!*

2. Open a command prompt. Navigate to D:\Setup\I386 (where D is the drive letter assigned to the CD-ROM drive).

> **QUESTION** *Why should you wait for replication to occur after ForestPrep?*

3. Issue the setup /domainprep command.

4. On the Microsoft Exchange Installation Wizard page, click Next.

5. On the License Agreement page, review the license, select I Agree, and then click Next.

6. On the Component Selection page, ensure that DomainPrep is shown beside the Microsoft Exchange component. Click Next.

7. The DomainPrep process begins. You are then presented with a message about insecure domains for mail-enabled groups.

> **QUESTION**   Which group should you remove members from to secure the domain for mail-enabled groups?

8. Click OK after reviewing the message. The DomainPrep process continues. When it is finished, click Finish and then log off.

EXERCISE 2.7: INSTALLING EXCHANGE SERVER 2003 IN A NEW EXCHANGE ORGANIZATION

Estimated completion time: 15 minutes

It is during the installation of the first Exchange Server 2003 computer that you decide on the type of installation and the Exchange Server 2003 organization name. In both the pilot program and the actual rollout, the installation of the first server can only occur once. As you cannot change the name of the organization, it is important that you get it right the first time.

> **IMPORTANT**   Complete the following tasks using Computerxx.

1. Log on using the Exchange.fulladmin account with the password P@ssw0rd.

2. Open a command prompt. Navigate to D:\Setup\I386 (where D is the drive letter assigned to the CD-ROM drive).

3. Type **setup** and press ENTER.

> **QUESTION**   What would happen if you tried to install Exchange using the Exchange.domainprep or Exchange.forestprep accounts?

4. On the Microsoft Exchange Installation Wizard page, click Next.

5. On the License Agreement page, review the license, select I Agree, and then click Next.

6. On the Component Selection page, leave the default values in place, and click Next.

7. On the Installation Type page, ensure that Create A New Exchange Organization is selected. Click Next.

8. In the Organization Name box, type **Contoso Exchange Pilot** as shown in Figure 2-7, and click Next.

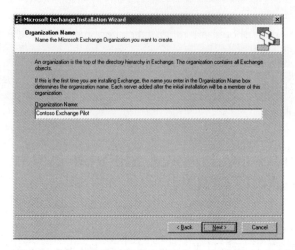

Figure 2-7 Configuring the new Exchange organization name

9. On the Licensing Agreement page, select I Agree And I Have Read And Will Be Bound By The License Agreement For This Product.

> **QUESTION**   You have 40 users who use 30 computers to access Exchange Server 2003. How many client access licenses must you purchase?

10. Review the installation summary, and click Next.

   The installation might take between five and ten minutes.

11. When the installation finishes, click Finish, and then log off the computer. You may be required to perform a restart.

EXERCISE 2.8: INSTALLING EXCHANGE SERVER 2003 IN AN EXISTING EXCHANGE ORGANIZATION

Estimated completion time: 15 minutes

It stands to reason that during the Contoso rollout all but one Exchange server installed will not be the first in the forest. Understanding the differences between installing the first Exchange Server 2003 server in the forest and installing the others is important. It is important that your team members be aware of this, as this is exactly what they will be doing once the rollout begins after the end of the pilot phase.

IMPORTANT *Complete the following tasks using Computeryy.*

1. Log on using the exchange.fulladmin@contosoxx.com account with the password P@ssw0rd.

   If you have trouble logging on, ensure that you have completed Exercise 2.1 in its entirety.

2. Open a command prompt. Navigate to D:\Setup\I386 (where D is the drive letter assigned to the CD-ROM drive).

3. Type **setup** and press ENTER.

4. On the Microsoft Exchange Installation Wizard page, click Next.

5. On the License Agreement page, review the license, select I Agree, and then click Next.

6. On the Component Selection page, leave the default values in place, and click Next.

7. On the Licensing Agreement page, select I Agree And I Have Read And Will Be Bound By The License Agreement For This Product. Click Next.

   QUESTION *What differences do you notice between installing the first Exchange Server 2003 computer and installing the second one?*

8. Review the installation summary, and then click Next.

   The installation might take some time.

9. When the installation finishes, click Finish, and then log off the computer.

REVIEW QUESTIONS

Estimated completion time: 15 minutes
1. In your own words, describe what you learned during this lab.

2. Of which groups must the account used to run ForestPrep be a member?

3. Of which groups must the account used to run DomainPrep be a member?

4. After ForestPrep and DomainPrep are completed, what pre-existing conditions must the account that is used to actually install the first instance of Exchange Server 2003 in the forest meet?

5. Why aren't you given the option of creating a new organization when installing Exchange Server 2003 server in a forest where an alternate domain has an existing Exchange Server 2003 installation?

LAB CHALLENGE 2.1: IDENTIFYING THE NEW GROUPS AND NEW USER PROPERTIES CREATED BY DOMAINPREP

Estimated completion time: 10 minutes

One of the most significant modifications that occurs once Exchange Server 2003 is installed is to the user properties. To explore this as a part of the pilot program, you want to create a new mailbox-enabled user and compare that user's properties with those of an older user.

> **IMPORTANT**   Complete the following tasks on Computerxx and Computeryy.

■ Using the Active Directory Users And Computers console, make a list of all new groups and new user properties created by DomainPrep. To help you do this, create a new user called Exchange.testuser that has an Exchange mailbox using the default settings. Compare these properties to that of an existing user such as Exchange.domainprep.

■ Perform these activities using the Exchange.fulladmin user account.

LAB CHALLENGE 2.2: IDENTIFYING NEW SERVICES INSTALLED WITH EXCHANGE SERVER 2003

Another significant modification that occurs once Exchange Server 2003 is installed is to the list of installed services.

> **IMPORTANT**   Complete the following tasks on Computerxx and Computeryy.

■ Generate a list of the new services that have been installed on Windows Server 2003 due to the installation of Exchange Server 2003, and determine which are configured to automatically start.

LAB 3
CONFIGURING A MICROSOFT EXCHANGE SERVER 2003 INFRASTRUCTURE

This lab contains the following exercises and activities:

- Exercise 3.1: Preparing Groups for the Delegation of Administrative Roles

- Exercise 3.2: Exploring the Basic Functionality of Exchange System Manager

- Exercise 3.3: The Delegation of Control Wizard

- Exercise 3.4: Exploring Administrative Roles

- Exercise 3.5: Adding and Removing Exchange Server 2003 Components

- Review Questions

- Lab Challenge 3.1: Configuring New Administrative and Routing Groups and switching from Mixed Mode to Native Mode

SCENARIO

The goal of the third stage of the Contoso Exchange Pilot Program is to familiarize your team with administrative roles, Exchange System Manager, and the installation and removal of Microsoft Exchange Server 2003 components. Unlike previous stages of the pilot program, which involved preliminary tasks like server preparation and software installation, from stage three onward you will be familiarizing yourself with aspects of Exchange that you and the members of your team eventually will use on a daily basis.

After completing this lab, you will be able to:

- Delegate administrative roles.

- Identify important areas of Exchange System Manager.

- Add and remove Exchange Server 2003 components.

- Switch from mixed mode to native mode.

- Create routing and administrative groups.

Estimated lesson time: 110 minutes

BEFORE YOU BEGIN

To successfully complete this lab, you will need the following:

- Two networked computers with Microsoft Windows Server 2003 installed using stand-alone configuration according to the setup guide

- Windows Server 2003 CD

- Exchange Server 2003 Enterprise Edition CD

- To have completed all exercises in Labs 1 and 2

> **IMPORTANT**   This lab is written to be performed on two computers. If each student has only a single computer, students can work as partners and share computers when needed. The first computer will be Computerxx, and the second computer will be Computeryy. Computerxx typically has an odd-numbered name, such as Computer01 and Computer03. Computeryy typically has an even-numbered name, such as Computer02 and Computer04. If you are unsure of your computer's name, open a command prompt window and run the hostname command to find out.

EXERCISE 3.1: PREPARING GROUPS FOR THE DELEGATION OF ADMINISTRATIVE ROLES

Estimated completion time: 15 minutes

This stage of the pilot program requires you to create a set of test users and groups. Once created, you will use these test users and groups to demonstrate the various aspects of Exchange Administration covered in this lab. As you and the members of your team are all experienced Windows Server 2003 administrators, creating the users and groups needed for this stage of the pilot program should pose little difficulty.

> **IMPORTANT**   Complete the following tasks on Computerxx and Computeryy.

1. Log on with the Administrator account. The password is **P@ssw0rd** or one assigned to you by your lab proctor.

2. From the Administrative Tools menu, open Active Directory Users And Computers.

3. In the Users container, create the following three global groups:

   Exchange.Admins

   Exchange.Full.Admins

   Exchange.View.Only

   > **QUESTION**   If you wanted to create only three groups for the entire forest to delegate the three Exchange roles to, which group type would you create and why?

4. If presented the option, do not create an Exchange e-mail address for the groups.

   > **QUESTION**   What is the difference between security and distribution groups?

5. On Computer*xx* create the users listed in the following table and add them to the corresponding groups. Set each user's password to P@ssw0rd, and make sure the passwords never expire. Allow an Exchange mailbox to be created. Set the Server and Mailbox Store of each user to Computer*xx*.

Username	Logon Name	Groups
Jay Adams	j.adams	Administrators, exchange.full.admins
Michael Alexander	m.alexander	Administrators, exchange.admins
John Arthur	j.arthur	Backup Operators, exchange.view.only

6. On Computer*yy* create the users listed in the following table and add them to the corresponding groups. Set each user's password to P@ssw0rd, and make sure the passwords never expire. Do not allow an Exchange mailbox to be created.

Username	Logon Name	Groups
Dan Bacon	d.bacon	Administrators, exchange.full.admins
Bryan Baker	b.baker	Administrators, exchange.admins
Adam Barr	a.barr	Backup Operators, exchange.view.only

EXERCISE 3.2: EXPLORING THE BASIC FUNCTIONALITY OF EXCHANGE SYSTEM MANAGER

Estimated completion time: 20 minutes

Exchange System Manager is the primary administrative tool used to manage Exchange Server 2003. To familiarize your team with this tool, you navigate through certain useful areas of Exchange System Manager. In later parts of the pilot program, you will explore other functions in greater depth. At this introductory stage, you are just providing basic familiarity by having your team members navigate to specific areas to complete common Exchange tasks.

> **IMPORTANT**   Complete the following tasks on Computerxx and Computeryy.

1. Log on with the exchange.fulladmin@contosoxx.com account. The password is P@ssw0rd.

2. Select System Manager from the Microsoft Exchange program group. This opens Exchange System Manager.

3. Right-click Contoso Exchange Pilot (Exchange), and select Properties.

4. Select the Display Routing Groups and Display Administrative Groups check boxes as shown in Figure 3-1.

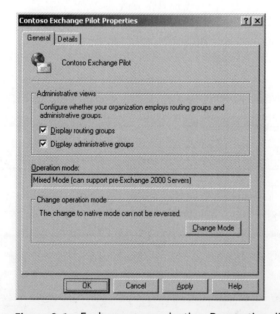

Figure 3-1   Exchange organization Properties dialog box

5. Click OK to close the Contoso Exchange Pilot Properties dialog box.

> **QUESTION**   What alert is issued when you click OK?

6. Restart Exchange System Manager by closing it and then opening it again.

7. Click the plus sign to open the Global Settings node.

8. Right-click the Internet Message Formats node to view MIME content types as shown in Figure 3-2.

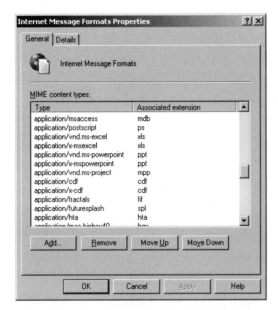

Figure 3-2   Internet Message Formats Properties dialog box

9. Click OK to close the Properties dialog box.

10. Right-click the Message Delivery node, and select Properties. Click the Defaults tab.

> **QUESTION**   By default, what is the maximum number of recipients to whom a message will be delivered?

11. Click OK to close the Message Delivery Properties dialog box.

12. Expand the Administrative Groups node. Expand the First Administrative Group node.

13. Expand the Routing Groups node, and then expand the First Routing Group node.

> **QUESTION**   What is the difference between an administrative group and a routing group?

14. Close Exchange System Manager.

EXERCISE 3.3: THE DELEGATION OF CONTROL WIZARD

Estimated completion time: 10 minutes

The Delegation of Control Wizard can be used only by a user delegated the Exchange Full Administrator role. Through this wizard you can delegate one of three roles: Exchange Full Administrator, Exchange Administrator, and Exchange View Only Administrator. In this exercise, rather than using this wizard each time you wish to change a member of your team's role, you create a set of security groups and delegate the roles to these security groups. To give users particular roles, you need to add them to the relevant security group rather than run the Exchange Administration Delegation Wizard. Another advantage of this approach is that you can use the restricted groups functionality of group policy to limit the group membership to approved staff only.

> **IMPORTANT** Complete the following tasks on Computerxx and Computeryy.

1. Log on with the exchange.fulladmin@contosoxx.com account. The password is P@ssw0rd or one assigned to you by your lab proctor.

2. Right-click the Contoso Exchange Pilot (Exchange) node, and select Delegate Control. This starts the Exchange Administration Delegation Wizard (see Figure 3-3). Click Next.

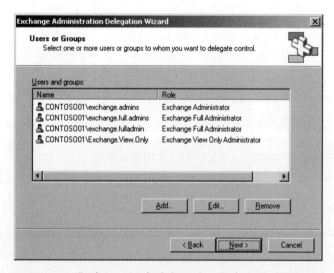

Figure 3-3   Exchange Administration Delegation Wizard

3. Click Add. On Computerxx, delegate the contosoxx\exchange.admins group the Exchange Administrator role, the contosoxx\exchange. view.only group the Exchange View Only Administrator role, and the contosoxx\exchange.full.admins group the Exchange Full Administrator role. On Computeryy, delegate the contosoyy\exchange.

admins group the Exchange Administrator role, the contosoyy\
exchange.view.only group the Exchange View Only Administrator
role, and the contosoyy\exchange.full.admins group the Exchange
Full Administrator role.

4. When you have finished, click Next, and then click Finish. After you
   click finish, you are presented with a message. Read the message, and
   then click OK.

   QUESTION   What did the message say?

5. Close Exchange System Manager, and log off.

EXERCISE 3.4: EXPLORING ADMINISTRATIVE ROLES

Estimated completion time: 25 minutes

As mentioned earlier, different members of your team will require different administrative access to Exchange Server 2003. For this exercise you test how different administrative roles limit functionality within Exchange System Manager. You explore how a user delegated one role has permission to do some things but not others, whereas a user with another delegated role has a different set of permissions.

   IMPORTANT   Complete the following tasks on Computerxx and
   Computeryy.

1. Log on to Computerxx with the j.arthur account. Then log on to Computeryy with the a.barr account. The password is P@ssw0rd.

   QUESTION   Why are the j.arthur and a.barr users able to log on to the
   domain controllers hosting Exchange Server 2003 when their accounts
   are not members of the local administrators groups?

2. Right-click the First Administrative Group node under the Administrative Groups node. Select Delegate Control.

3. The Exchange Administration Delegation Wizard opens. Click Next,
   then click Add. On Computerxx, delegate the Exchange Full Administrator role to the j.arthur user account. On Computeryy, delegate the
   Exchange Full Administrator role to the a.barr user account.

4. Click Next, and then click Finish. Read the message. Click OK.

   QUESTION   What does the message say, and what does it mean?

5. Navigate to the Queues node (see Figure 3-4), located under the Computer*xx* node, located under the Servers node, located under the First Administrative Group.

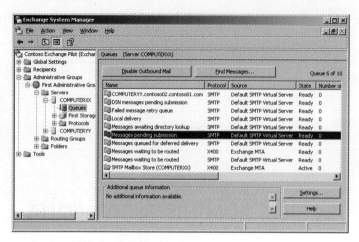

Figure 3-4   The Queues node

6. Right-click the Messages Pending Submission queue, and select Freeze. Note the error message.

7. Close Exchange System Manager, and log off.

8. Log on to Computer*xx* with the m.alexander account. Log on to Computer*yy* with the b.baker account. The password is P@ssw0rd.

9. Open Exchange System Manager.

10. Right-click the First Administrative Group node, and select Delegate Control.

11. The Exchange Administration Delegation Wizard opens. Click Next, then click Add. On Computer*xx*, delegate the Exchange Administrator role to the j.arthur user account. On Computer*yy*, delegate the Exchange Administrator role to the a.barr user account.

12. Click Next, and then click Finish. Read the message. Click OK.

13. Navigate to the Queues node, located under the Computer*xx* node.

14. Right-click the Messages Pending Submission queue, and select Freeze.

> **QUESTION**   What is the difference between being delegated the Exchange View Only Administrator role and the Exchange Administrator role in relation to the management of queues?

15. Right-click the Messages Pending Submission queue, and select Unfreeze.

16. Close all open windows on both computers and log off.

EXERCISE 3.5: ADDING AND REMOVING EXCHANGE SERVER 2003 COMPONENTS

Estimated completion time: 20 minutes

In certain situations it may be necessary to add and remove components from Exchange Server 2003 computers once the system has been put into full production – for example, installing the Calendar Connector component to allow Exchange users to access the calendars of users in a partner organization that uses Lotus Notes. To train your staff for this possibility, this part of the pilot program will have you examine the process of adding and removing components from Exchange Server 2003.

> **IMPORTANT**   Complete the following tasks on Computerxx and Computeryy.

1. Log on with the exchange.fulladmin@contosoxx.com account. The password is P@ssw0rd or one assigned to you by your lab proctor.

2. Confirm that the Exchange Server 2003 installation media is in the CD-ROM drive.

3. Open a command prompt, and navigate to the \Setup\i386 folder on the CD-ROM drive.

4. From the prompt, issue the setup command. When the Microsoft Exchange Server Installation Wizard appears, click Next.

5. On the Component Selection page, shown in Figure 3-5, click the Microsoft Exchange drop-down list, and select Change.

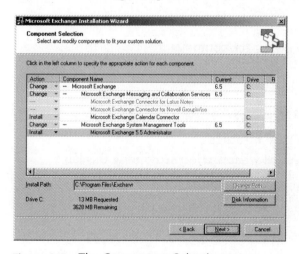

Figure 3-5   The Component Selection page

6. Click the Microsoft Exchange Messaging And Collaboration Services drop-down list, and select Change.

7. Click the Microsoft Exchange Calendar Connector drop-down list, and select Install.

8. Click the Microsoft Exchange System Management Tools drop-down list, and select Change.

9. Click the Microsoft Exchange 5.5 Administrator drop-down list, and select Install.

10. Click Next to add these components to Exchange Server 2003.

11. Click Next again on the Installation Summary page.

12. The Component Progress page is displayed while the newly selected components are being installed. When it finishes, click Finish.

13. Open the Microsoft Exchange program group, and verify that Exchange 5.5 Administrator is installed.

14. From the command prompt, issue the setup command again.

15. On the Component Selection page, use the technique detailed in steps 5 through 9, this time removing the Microsoft Exchange Calendar Connector and the Microsoft Exchange 5.5 Administrator components. Be careful to remove these components only and not Exchange Server 2003 itself.

16. Click Next twice, and then click Finish.

17. Open the Microsoft Exchange program group, and verify that Exchange 5.5 Administrator is no longer installed, but that Exchange System Manager remains present.

18. Close all windows, and log off the computer.

REVIEW QUESTIONS

Estimated completion time: 20 minutes
1. In your own words, describe what you learned during this lab.

2. Which MIME content type is associated with the .spl, .tgz, and .dir extensions in the Internet Message Formats node?

3. What is the default size limit, in kilobytes (KB), of messages that can be received by a user with a mailbox on an Exchange Server 2003 computer?

4. Under what conditions can you move Exchange Server 2003 computers between routing groups and administrative groups?

5. What tasks can a user delegated the Exchange Full Administrator role perform that a user delegated the Exchange Administrator role cannot?

6. What is the difference between an administrative group and an administrative role?

LAB CHALLENGE 3.1: CONFIGURING NEW ADMINISTRATIVE AND ROUTING GROUPS AND SWITCHING FROM MIXED MODE TO NATIVE MODE

Estimated completion time: 40 minutes

Part of the pilot program involves assessing the knowledge that you have gained to this point. That includes performing small tasks that you don't have the full instructions for, but that you should be able to complete by using the knowledge you have gained during today's exercises. You should be able to:

> **IMPORTANT**   Complete the following tasks on Computerxx and Computeryy.

- On Computerxx, create a routing group named Routing_Groupxx. On Computeryy, create a routing group named Routing_Groupyy.

- On Computerxx, create a new administrative group named Admin-Groupxx. On Computeryy, create a new administrative group named AdminGroupyy. Provide a screenshot showing the newly created administrative and routing groups.

- On Computerxx, change the mode from native mode to mixed mode. Provide a screenshot showing the Contoso Exchange Pilot organization running in native mode.

> **QUESTION**   What is the difference between running an Exchange Server 2003 organization in mixed mode as opposed to running an Exchange Server 2003 organization in native mode?

- On Computerxx, delegate the Exchange Full Administrator role for the AdminGroupxx administrative group to a newly created security group named admin.groupxx. On Computeryy, delegate the Exchange Full Administrator role for the AdminGroupyy administrative group to a newly created security group named admin.groupyy.

LAB 4

INSTALLING MICROSOFT EXCHANGE SERVER 2003 CLUSTERS AND FRONT-END AND BACK-END SERVERS

This lab contains the following exercises and activities:

- Exercise 4.1: Creating a Network Load Balancing Cluster

- Exercise 4.2: Adding a Host to a Network Load Balancing Cluster

- Exercise 4.3: Verifying a Network Load Balancing Cluster

- Exercise 4.4: Removing a Network Load Balancing Cluster

- Exercise 4.5: Configuring a Back-End Server

- Exercise 4.6: Configuring a Front-End Server

- Exercise 4.7: Verifying Front-End Server Configuration

- Review Questions

- Lab Challenge 4.1: Restoring to Previous Configuration

SCENARIO

Now that you have provided the Contoso Exchange Pilot team with a basic understanding of Microsoft Exchange Server 2003 postinstallation configuration as well as Exchange System Manager, you briefly will explore network load balancing clusters and the configuration of Exchange in a front-end and back-end relationship.

It is important that your team understands network load balancing and the configuration of front-end and back-end relationships as eventually Contoso, Ltd. will use four network load balanced front-end servers to provide e-mail access using Microsoft Outlook Web Access to employees in remote locations.

After completing this lab, you will be able to:

- Create a network load balancing cluster.

- Add a server to an existing network load balancing cluster.

- Remove a network load balancing cluster.

- Determine which users have Exchange Server mailboxes on a particular Exchange Server.

- Move Exchange Server mailboxes from one server to another within an Exchange organization.

- Configure an Exchange Server 2003 computer as a front-end server.

Estimated lesson time: 110 minutes

BEFORE YOU BEGIN

To successfully complete this lab, you will need the following:

- Two networked computers with Microsoft Windows Server 2003 installed using stand-alone configuration according to the setup guide

- Windows Server 2003 CD

- Exchange Server 2003 Enterprise Edition CD

- To have completed all exercises in Labs 1, 2, and 3

> **NOTE**   This lab is written to be performed on two computers. If each student has only a single computer, students can work as partners and share computers when needed. The first computer will be Computerxx, and the second computer will be Computeryy. Computerxx typically has an odd-numbered name, such as Computer01 and Computer03. Computeryy typically has an even-numbered name, such as Computer02 and Computer04. If you are unsure of your computer's name, run a command prompt and run the hostname command to find out.

EXERCISE 4.1: CREATING A NETWORK LOAD BALANCING CLUSTER

Estimated completion time: 20 minutes

To begin exploring network load balancing, your team needs to first create a network load balancing cluster. In creating a cluster you must decide whether to use unicast or multicast methods of cluster communication, and you must decide on a cluster Internet Protocol (IP) address and create a dedicated fully qualified domain name (FQDN) for the cluster that maps to this address. One of the reasons you chose network load balancing is that it ships by default with Windows Server 2003. In configuring this pilot program network load balancing cluster, your team will become more familiar with the underlying technology and should be able to deploy it when it is time for the rollout.

> **IMPORTANT**   *Complete the following tasks on Computerxx.*

1. Log on with the account Administrator@contosoxx.com. The password is P@ssw0rd or one assigned to you by your lab proctor.

2. From the Administrative Tools menu, open Network Load Balancing Manager.

> **NOTE**   *If Network Load Balancing Manager does not appear in the Administrative Tools group, you might need to add the Network Load Balancing service to your computer. To add Network Load Balancing, in the Local Area Connection Properties dialog box, select Install, select Service, click Add, and then select Network Load Balancing.*

3. From the Cluster menu, select New.

4. In the Cluster Parameters dialog box, shown in Figure 4-1, in the IP Address text box, enter the cluster's IP address.

> **NOTE**   *The IP address of the cluster will be the IP address of Contosoxx plus 100. So if the IP address of Contosoxx is 10.1.1.15, the IP address of the cluster will be 10.1.1.115.*

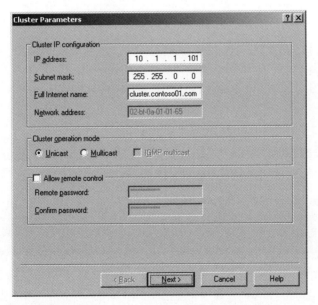

Figure 4-1   The Cluster Parameters dialog box

5. In the Subnet Mask text box, type **255.255.0.0**.

6. In the Full Internet Name text box, type **cluster.contoso*xx*.com**, where *xx* is the assigned number of Computer*xx*.

   This Full Internet Name is used by clients to access the cluster.

7. In the Cluster Operation Mode section, select Multicast, and then click Next.

8. In the Cluster IP Addresses dialog box, click Next.

9. In the Port Rules dialog box, click Next.

10. In the Connect dialog box, shown in Figure 4-2, in the Host text box, type **computer*xx*.contoso*xx*.com**, and then click Connect.

11. The Connection Status box displays Connected, and Computer*xx*'s network interface appears in the Interfaces Available For Configuring A New Cluster list.

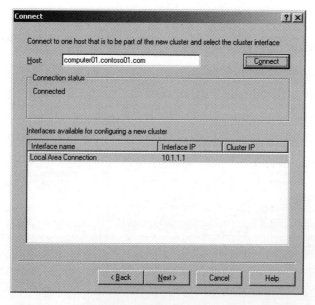

Figure 4-2   The Connect screen

12. In the Interfaces Available For Configuring A New Cluster list, select Local Area Connection, and then click Next.

13. In the Host Parameters dialog box, click Finish.

   A new cluster appears in the console tree. After about a minute, the hourglass disappears and your server status is listed as Converged. You can see your server's status by selecting the cluster, cluster.contoso*xx*.com, in the console tree and viewing the details pane.

14. Close the Network Load Balancing Manager console.

15. Open a command prompt and type the command **dnscmd / recordadd contosoxx.com cluster A 10.1.1.X** (where *X* is the IP address that you entered in step 4).

> **QUESTION** *What does the command issued at the command prompt do? What can you do to check that the command has executed successfully?*

16. Close all windows and log off Computer*xx*.

EXERCISE 4.2: ADDING A HOST TO A NETWORK LOAD BALANCING CLUSTER

Estimated completion time: 15 minutes

Now that a cluster has been configured, it is time to add a second node. The second node in this case is the other Exchange Server 2003 computer used for the Contoso pilot program.

> **IMPORTANT** *Complete the following tasks on Computeryy. Ensure that Exercise 4.1 is completed on Computerxx before attempting Exercise 4.2.*

1. Log on with the account Administrator@contoso*xx*.com.

2. From the Administrative Tools menu, open Network Load Balancing Manager.

> **NOTE** *If Network Load Balancing Manager does not appear in the Administrative Tools group, you might need to add the Network Load Balancing service to your computer. To add Network Load Balancing, in the Local Area Connection Properties dialog box, select Install, select Service, click Add, and then select Network Load Balancing.*

3. From the Cluster menu, select Connect To Existing.

4. In the Connect dialog box, in the Host box, type **computerxx. contosoxx.com**, and then click Connect.

5. In the Clusters list, select cluster.contoso*xx*.com, and then click Finish.

> **QUESTION** *Why can't you use the administrator@contosoyy.contosoxx.com account to perform this function?*

6. In the Network Load Balancing Manager console tree, right-click cluster.contoso*xx*.com, and select Add Host To Cluster.

7. In the Connect dialog box, in the Host box, type **computer*yy*.contoso*yy*.contoso*xx*.com**, and then click Connect.

8. In the Interfaces Available For Configuring The Cluster list, select Local Area Connection, and then click Next.

9. In the Host Parameters dialog box, click Finish.

    A new host appears in the cluster in the console tree. After about a minute, the hourglass disappears and your server status is listed as Converged. You can see your server's status by selecting the cluster, cluster.contoso*xx*.com, in the console tree and viewing the details pane.

10. Open a command prompt, and ping host cluster.contoso*xx*.com.

    QUESTION   What IP address is returned when you ping host cluster.contoso*xx*.com?

11. Close all open windows, and log off.

EXERCISE 4.3: VERIFYING A NETWORK LOAD BALANCING CLUSTER

Estimated completion time: 15 minutes

Although Network Load Balancing Manager informs the Exchange pilot program team that the two-node cluster is indeed functional, you have decided to test whether or not this is actually the case. Rather than configuring Post Office Protocol version 3 (POP3) or Internet Message Access Protocol version 4 (IMAP4) clients, you have decided to use Outlook Web Access, the technology that will be clustered during the rollout of Exchange Server 2003 across the Contoso organization. Outlook Web Access provides an Outlook-like interface and can be run through Microsoft Internet Explorer, meaning little extra configuration is required.

IMPORTANT   Complete the following tasks on Computer*yy*.

1. Log on to Computer*yy* with the account b.baker@contoso*yy*.contoso*xx*.com. Use the password P@ssw0rd.

2. Open Active Directory Users And Computers.

> **NOTE**   You did not create Exchange mailboxes for these users when you created them in Lab 3. You do so now for the purposes of testing clustering.

3. By holding down the Ctrl key, select Adam Barr, Bryan Baker, and Dan Bacon's user accounts. Right-click and select Exchange Tasks. This launches the Exchange Tasks Wizard. Click Next.

4. Select Create Mailbox, and then click Next.

5. Ensure that the server is set to Contosoyy and that the mailbox store is located on Contosoyy. Click Next, and then click Finish.

6. Close all windows and log off.

> **IMPORTANT**   Complete the following tasks on Computerxx. If your lab partner is using Computeryy, he or she can proceed directly to step 21.

7. Log on to Computerxx as administrator@contosoxx.com.

8. Open Internet Explorer, and click OK at the Internet Explorer Enhanced Security Configuration message.

9. Enter the URL *http://computeryy.contosoyy.contosoxx.com/exchange* in the address bar.

10. Enter the login credentials **m.alexander@contosoxx.com** in the Authentication dialog box.

11. Note that the Authentication dialog box asks again for credentials, this time for a different server. Retype m.alexander's credentials.

12. Click Add twice to add this to your list of trusted sites. Click Close.

13. Click OK at the IE Enhanced Security Configuration message.

14. Note that you have been redirected to Computerxx rather than Computeryy.

> **QUESTION**   Why have you been redirected from Computeryy to Computerxx?

15. Close and then reopen Internet Explorer. Click OK at the Internet Explorer Enhanced Security Configuration message.

16. Enter the URL *http://cluster.contosoxx.com/exchange*.

17. Enter the login credentials **m.alexander@contosoxx.com** in the Authentication dialog box.

18. Click Add twice to add this to your list of trusted sites. Click Close.

19. Click OK at the IE Enhanced Security Configuration message.

> **QUESTION** What is the difference between accessing the server's FQDN and the cluster's FQDN?

20. Close all windows, and log off Computerxx.

> **IMPORTANT** Complete the following tasks on Computeryy. If you are working without a lab partner, proceed directly to Exercise 4.4.

21. Log on to Computeryy as administrator@contosoyy.contosoxx.com.

22. Open Internet Explorer, and click OK at the Internet Explorer Enhanced Security Configuration message.

23. Enter the URL *http://computerxx.contosoxx.com/exchange* in the address bar.

24. Enter the login credentials **a.barr@contosoyy.contosoxx.com** in the Authentication dialog box.

25. Note that the Authentication dialog box asks again for credentials, this time for a different server. Retype a.barr's credentials.

26. Click Add twice to add this to your list of trusted sites. Click Close.

27. Click OK at the IE Enhanced Security Configuration message.

28. Note that you have been redirected to Computeryy rather than Computerxx.

> **QUESTION** Why have you been redirected from Computerxx to Computeryy?

29. Close and then re-open Internet Explorer. Click OK at the Internet Explorer Enhanced Security Configuration message.

30. Enter the URL *http://cluster.contosoxx.com/exchange*.

31. Enter the login credentials **a.barr@contosoyy.contosoxx.com** in the Authentication dialog box.

32. Click Add twice to add this to your list of trusted sites. Click Close.

33. Click OK at the IE Enhanced Security Configuration message.

> **QUESTION**   What is the difference between accessing the server's FQDN and the cluster's FQDN?

34. Close all windows, and log off Computeryy.

EXERCISE 4.4: REMOVING A NETWORK LOAD BALANCING CLUSTER

Estimated completion time: 5 minutes

As the next phase of the pilot program involves exploring front-end and back-end configurations, you need to tear down the existing network load balancing cluster so that you can reconfigure the two Exchange Server 2003 computers into this new relationship.

> **IMPORTANT**   Complete the following tasks on Computerxx.

1. Log on with the Administrator account. The password is P@ssw0rd or one assigned to you by your lab proctor.

2. From the Administrative Tools menu, open Network Load Balancing Manager. Click OK to the warning message.

3. From the Cluster menu, select Connect To Existing.

4. In the Connect dialog box, enter the host as **localhost**, click Connect, and then click Finish.

5. Select cluster.contosoxx.com, and then from the Cluster menu select Delete.

6. Read the warning message, and then click Yes.

> **QUESTION**   What does the warning message inform you will happen?

7. Wait several moments while the cluster is reconfigured. Close the windows when the hourglasses disappear and the cluster is removed from Network Load Balancing Manager.

8. Verify that the cluster has been removed by opening a command prompt and pinging cluster.contosoxx.com.

EXERCISE 4.5: CONFIGURING A BACK-END SERVER

Estimated completion time: 10 minutes

Back-end servers require no special configuration. They are essentially just normal Exchange Server 2003 computers that have requests routed to them by front-end servers rather than directly by clients. For the Contoso pilot program, you need to move all mailboxes to the server that will function as the back end. This is a relatively simple task that can be accomplished using the Active Directory Users And Computers console.

> **IMPORTANT**   Both you and your lab partner should complete the following tasks on Computerxx.

1. Log on with the Administrator account. The password is P@ssw0rd or one assigned to you by your lab proctor.

2. Open Active Directory Users And Computers. Right-click Contosoxx.com, and then select Find.

3. In the Find Users, Contacts, And Groups dialog box, in the Find list, select Exchange Recipients.

4. On the General tab, shown in Figure 4-3, clear all check boxes except Users With Exchange Mailbox.

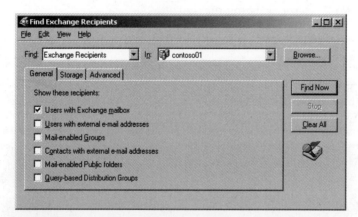

Figure 4-3   The Find Exchange Recipients dialog box

5. Click the Storage tab. Select Mailboxes On This Server, and then click Browse.

6. In the Select Exchange Server dialog box, type **Computerxx**, and then click OK.

7. In the Find Exchange Recipients dialog box, click Find Now.

A list of all users who have an Exchange Server 2003 mailbox on Computer*xx* is displayed.

8. Using the Ctrl key and the mouse, select all users except System Mailbox.

9. Right-click the users, and select Exchange Tasks.

10. In the Exchange Task Wizard, click Next.

11. On the Available Tasks page, select Move Mailbox, and then click Next.

12. On the Move Mailbox page, in the Server list, verify that Contoso Exchange Pilot/First Administrative Group/Computer*yy* is selected.

13. In the Mailbox Store list, verify that First Storage Group/Mailbox Store (Computer*yy*) is selected, and then click Next.

14. On the Move Mailbox page, click Next.

15. On the Task Schedule page, click Next.

16. The Task In Progress page appears showing the status of the mailbox move.

17. When the move is complete, review the summary, and then click Finish.

18. Close the Find Exchange Recipients dialog box.

19. Close Active Directory Users And Computers.

> **QUESTION**   What method could you use to verify that all mailboxes have indeed been transferred to Computer*yy*?

20. Close all open windows.

EXERCISE 4.6: CONFIGURING A FRONT-END SERVER

Estimated completion time: 15 minutes

The final step required before configuring a server as a front end is to move any Recipient Update Services and Offline Address Lists that are hosted on the prospective front-end server to a back-end server. Once this task is completed, it is relatively simple to convert a server to Front End mode. Once the conversion is done, Exchange services need to be restarted. This can be done manually or by rebooting the system.

> **IMPORTANT**   Both you and your lab partner should complete the following tasks on Computer*xx*.

1. Log on with the exchange.fulladmin@contosoxx.com account.

2. Open Exchange System Manager, and browse to Recipient Update Services.

3. Edit the properties of each of the Recipient Update Services that use Computerxx as the host Exchange server, changing that server to Computeryy.

4. Browse to Offline Address Lists.

5. Edit the properties of the Default Offline Address List so that it is hosted on Exchange Server Computeryy rather than Computerxx.

6. Browse to Administrative Groups\First Administrative Group\ Servers\Computerxx.

7. In the console tree, right-click Computerxx, and then select Properties.

8. In the Computerxx Properties dialog box, shown in Figure 4-4, select the This Is A Front-End Server check box, and then click OK.

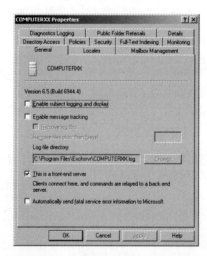

Figure 4-4   Configuring a front-end server

9. In the warning dialog box, click OK to acknowledge that the Computerxx server's POP, IMAP, Hypertext Transfer Protocol (HTTP), and Exchange services must be stopped and restarted, and that Secure Sockets Layer (SSL) should be configured to secure data transmissions between clients and the front-end server.

10. Restart Computerxx.

EXERCISE 4.7: VERIFYING FRONT-END SERVER CONFIGURATION

Estimated completion time: 10 minutes

Now that the pilot project servers are configured in a front-end and back-end relationship, you need to test that the configuration has been performed correctly. You do this by verifying that you can access mailboxes originally hosted on Computer*xx* and Computer*yy* through the Outlook Web Access server on Computer*xx*.

> **IMPORTANT** Complete the following tasks on Computer*xx* and Computer*yy*.

1. Log on to Computer*xx* using administrator@contoso*xx*.com. Log on to Computer*yy* using administrator@contoso*yy*.contoso*xx*.com.

2. Open Internet Explorer. Click OK at the Internet Explorer Enhanced Security Configuration message.

3. Navigate to *http://localhost/exchange/m.alexander*. Enter the password when required.

4. Navigate to *http://localhost/exchange/a.barr*. Enter the password when required.

> **QUESTION** How do you know that Computer*xx* is acting as a front-end server?

REVIEW QUESTIONS

Estimated completion time: 20 minutes

1. In your own words, describe what you learned during this lab.

2. What is the difference between specifying unicast and multicast as the cluster operation mode when configuring the parameters of a new cluster in Network Load Balancing Manager?

3. In the Move Mailbox Wizard, why is there an option to schedule the move for a later time and date?

4. List all of the services that must be restarted when Exchange Server 2003 is configured as a front-end server.

LAB CHALLENGE 4.1: RESTORING TO PREVIOUS CONFIGURATION

Estimated completion time: 40 minutes

Part of the pilot program involves assessing the knowledge that you have gained to this point. That includes performing small tasks which you don't have the full instructions for, but which you should be able to complete by using the knowledge you have gained during today's exercises. Although Contoso will be using network load balanced front-end servers during the eventual rollout, the rest of the pilot program revolves around the two Exchange Server 2003 computers not being configured in this manner. To continue the pilot program, you return Computerxx to its original configuration.

> **IMPORTANT**   Complete the following tasks on Computerxx and Computeryy.

- Configure Computerxx so that it is no longer a front-end server.
- Return all of the mailboxes that you moved from Computerxx to Computeryy back to Computerxx.
- Return the Recipient Update Service (Enterprise Configuration) to Computerxx.
- Return the Default Offline Address List to Computerxx.

TROUBLESHOOTING ADMINISTRATIVE DELEGATION AND EXCHANGE CONFIGURATION

Troubleshooting Lab A is a practical application of the knowledge you acquired from Labs 1 through 4. Your instructor or lab assistant has changed your computer configuration, causing it to "break." Your task in this lab is to apply your acquired skills to troubleshoot and resolve the break. A scenario is presented that lays out the parameters of the break and the conditions that must be met for the scenario to be resolved. This troubleshooting lab has two break scenarios. The first break scenario involves administrative delegation, and the second involves Microsoft Exchange Server 2003 configuration.

> **NOTE** **Do Not Proceed with This Lab Until You Receive Guidance from Your Instructor**   The break scenario that you will be performing will depend on which computer you are using. The first computer will be Computerxx, and the second computer will be Computeryy. Computerxx typically has an odd-numbered name, such as Computer01 and Computer03. Computeryy typically has an even-numbered name, such as Computer02 and Computer04. If you are unsure of your computer's name, run a command prompt and issue the hostname command. If you are using Computerxx, you will perform Break Scenario 1. If you are using Computeryy, you will perform Break Scenario 2. Your instructor or lab assistant might also have special instructions. Consult with your instructor before proceeding.

BREAK SCENARIO 1

IMPORTANT   *Perform this break scenario on Computerxx.*

When Exchange Server 2003 is deployed across Contoso, Ltd., policy will be that Exchange administrative roles will only be delegated to groups and not individual users.

- David Hamilton and Jim Hance are members of the Exchange.Admins group, which has been delegated the Exchange Administrator role. However neither of these users is able to perform Exchange Administrator duties, such as being able to create new administrative groups.

- Mark Hanson and Keith Harris should only have the Exchange View Only Administrator role. However both of these users are able to dismount the Mailbox Store on Computerxx and create new administrative groups.

- Before you check any solution, issue the gpupdate /force command from the command prompt.

- No new delegations should be made, and only the user and groups listed here should be delegated Exchange administrative roles.

User or Group	Role
Contosoxx\exchange.admins	Exchange Administrator
Contosoxx\exchange.full.admins	Exchange Full Administrator
Contosoxx\exchange.fulladmin	Exchange Full Administrator
Contosoxx\exchange.view.only	Exchange View Only Administrator
Contosoyy\exchange.admins	Exchange Administrator
Contosoyy\exchange.full.admins	Exchange Full Administrator
Contosoyy\exchange.view.only	Exchange View Only Administrator

As you resolve the problem, fill out the worksheet in the TroubleshootingLabA folder and include the following information:

- Description of the problem
- A list of all steps taken to diagnose the problem, even the ones that did not work
- Description of the exact issue and solution
- A list of the tools and resources you used to help solve this problem

BREAK SCENARIO 2

IMPORTANT   *Perform this break scenario on Computeryy.*

A credentialed administrator should be able to log on to any Exchange Server 2003 computer within the Contoso organization and manage any other Exchange Server 2003 computer. Currently you are unable to do this on Computeryy. Computeryy is exhibiting the following symptom:

- When you log on to Computeryy with the Administrator account, you are unable to access Exchange System Manager.

You need to perform the following task on Computeryy using the Administrator account:

- Create a new administrative group named Troubleshooting-A.

As you resolve the problem, fill out the worksheet in the TroubleshootingLabA folder and include the following information:

- Description of the problem

- A list of all steps taken to diagnose the problem, even the ones that did not work

- Description of the exact issue and solution

- A list of the tools and resources you used to help solve this problem

LAB 5
MANAGING RECIPIENT OBJECTS AND ADDRESS LISTS

This lab contains the following exercises and activities:

- Exercise 5.1: Creating and Initializing User Mailboxes

- Exercise 5.2: Mail-Enabling Contacts

- Exercise 5.3: Creating a Mail-Enabled Distribution Group

- Exercise 5.4: Deleting and Reconnecting Mailboxes

- Exercise 5.5: Configuring Storage Limits on Individual Mailboxes

- Exercise 5.6: Creating a Query-Based Distribution Group

- Exercise 5.7: Creating a New Storage Group and Mailbox Store

- Exercise 5.8: Moving a Storage Group

- Exercise 5.9: Creating an Offline Address List

- Exercise 5.10: Creating a New Recipient Policy

- Review Questions

- Lab Challenge 5.1: Moving a Database Store

- Lab Challenge 5.2: Changing a Mail Retention Policy

SCENARIO

Now that the basics of the Contoso Exchange Server 2003 pilot program are out of the way, it is time to get to the more routine daily activities that those working with Microsoft Exchange Server 2003 will be expected to carry out. These daily activities involve the creation, care, and maintenance of user mailboxes, storage groups, and address lists. It is important for your team to know how to create a mailbox, where to put it, how to remove it, and how to reconnect it if it is accidentally deleted. For all that they have learned about installation and configuration, 90 percent of your team's time will ultimately be taken up directly by tasks related to user mailboxes.

After completing this lab, you will be able to:

- Create and manage mailboxes.
- Mail-enable recipient objects.
- Configure storage limits on mailboxes.
- Configure permissions on mailboxes and distribution groups.
- Create query-based distribution groups.
- Manage storage groups and stores.
- Create offline address lists.
- Create recipient policies.

Estimated lesson time: 125 minutes

BEFORE YOU BEGIN

To successfully complete this lab, you will need the following:

- Two networked computers with Windows Server 2003 installed using stand-alone configuration according to the setup guide.
- Windows Server 2003 CD.
- Exchange Server 2003 Enterprise Edition CD.
- To have completed all exercises and lab challenges in Labs 1, 2, and 3. If you have performed Lab 4, ensure that all exercises and lab challenges have been completed.

IMPORTANT   This lab is written to be performed on two computers. If each student has only a single computer, students can work as partners and share computers when needed. The first computer will be Computerxx, and the second computer will be Computeryy. Computerxx typically has an odd-numbered name, such as Computer01 and Computer03. Computeryy typically has an even-numbered name, such as Computer02 and Computer04. If you are unsure of your computer's name, run a command prompt and issue the hostname command to find out. Unless otherwise specified, all user accounts used in this lab use the password P@ssw0rd.

EXERCISE 5.1: CREATING AND INITIALIZING USER MAILBOXES

Estimated completion time: 10 minutes

The first aspect of this phase of the pilot program is to show your team how to create an Exchange Server 2003 mailbox in conjunction with the process of creating a user account. You also will show them how to verify that the user's mailbox actually exists after it has been initialized.

> **IMPORTANT** *Complete the following tasks on Computerxx.*

1. Log on to Computer*xx* with the exchange.fulladmin user account. The password is P@ssw0rd or one assigned to you by your lab proctor.

2. Open Exchange System Manager. From the Action menu, click Delegate Control. Click Next.

3. Click Add. Click Browse. In the Enter The Object Name To Select box type **Administrator@contosoxx.com**. Click OK.

4. On the Role drop-down list, select Exchange Administrator. Click OK.

5. Click Add. Click Browse. In the Enter The Object Name To Select box type **Administrator@contosoyy.contosoxx.com**. Click OK.

6. On the Role drop-down list, select Exchange Administrator. Click OK.

7. Verify that the Administrator accounts for both the Contoso*xx* and Contoso*yy* domains have been assigned the Exchange Administrator role. Click Next.

8. Click Finish. Click OK to dismiss the information message.

9. Log off Computer*xx*.

> **IMPORTANT** *Complete the following tasks on Computerxx and Computeryy.*

10. Log on with the Administrator account. The password is P@ssw0rd or one assigned to you by your lab proctor.

11. Open Active Directory Users And Computers.

12. In the console tree, right-click Users, select New, and then click User.

13. In the New Object − User dialog box, type information into the boxes as follows, and then click Next.

In this box	Computerxx	Computeryy
First Name	Sharon	Chris
Initials	S	A
Last Name	Salavaria	Preston
User Logon Name	s.salavaria	c.preston

14. In the Password and Confirm Password boxes, type **P@ssw0rd**, clear the User Must Change Password At Next Logon check box, and then click Next.

15. Verify that the Create An Exchange Mailbox check box is selected. From the Server list, select Contoso Exchange Pilot/First Administrative Group/*YourServer*, where *YourServer* is either Computerxx or Computeryy. From the Mailbox Store list, select First Storage Group/ Mailbox Store (*YourServer*), and then click Next.

16. Click Finish to create the user account.

17. Open Exchange System Manager.

18. In Exchange System Manager, browse to Administrative Groups\First Administrative Group\Servers*YourServer*\First Storage Group\Mailbox Store (*YourServer*), and then click Mailboxes.

19. In the Mailboxes container, in the details pane, verify whether the mailbox for the user you just created (Sharon S. Salavaria or Chris A. Preston) appears.

> **QUESTION** Did the mailbox appear for your user in the Mailboxes container? If not, why?

20. Start Microsoft Internet Explorer. Click OK to the Internet Explorer Enhanced Security Configuration message. If using Computerxx, navigate to the URL *http://localhost/exchange/s.salavaria*. If using Computeryy, navigate to the URL *http://localhost/exchange/c.preston*.

21. When prompted, enter the appropriate user's authentication credentials.

22. In the Outlook Web Access window, on the toolbar, click New.

23. In the Untitled Message box, in the To box, type the name of the user you just created (**Sharon S. Salavaria** or **Chris A. Preston**).

24. In the Subject box, type **Initialize Mailbox Message**, and then click Send.

25. Switch to Exchange System Manager.

26. In the Mailboxes container, in the details pane, verify that the mailbox for the user you just created (Sharon S. Salavaria or Chris A. Preston) appears.

> **TIP** Be patient: you might need to refresh the view to update the Mailboxes container.

27. Close all open Windows.

EXERCISE 5.2: MAIL-ENABLING CONTACTS

Estimated completion time: 10 minutes

Mail-enabling contacts allows people who might work with your organization, such as contractors, who maintain an e-mail address on a mail server external to your organization, to appear in the Global Address List (GAL). As there are many such contractors working within Contoso, part of the pilot program deals with how to turn the contact information about them stored within Active Directory into an e-mail address accessible through the GAL.

> **IMPORTANT** Complete the following tasks on Computerxx and Computeryy.

1. Right-click the Users container within Active Directory Users And Computers, and select New Contact. Enter the contact details shown in the following table. Do not select the Create An Exchange E-mail Address option.

In this box	Computerxx	Computeryy
First Name	Josh	Andy
Last Name	Barnhill	Ruth
Full Name	Josh Barnhill	Andy Ruth
Display Name	Josh Barnhill	Andy Ruth

2. Once the contact is created, right-click the contact, and select Exchange Tasks.

3. In the Exchange Task Wizard, on the Welcome To The Exchange Task Wizard page, click Next.

4. On the Available Tasks page, verify that Establish E-Mail Address is selected, and then click Next.

5. On the Establish E-Mail Address page, click Modify.

6. In the New E-Mail Address dialog box, click SMTP Address, and then click OK.

7. In the Internet Address Properties dialog box, enter the e-mail addresses from the following table, and then click OK.

Contact Name	Josh Barnhill	Andy Ruth
E-Mail Address	JBarnhill@tailspintoys.msft	ARuth@tailspintoys.msft

8. On the Establish E-Mail Address page, shown in Figure 5-1, click Next.

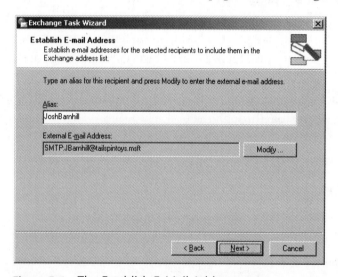

Figure 5-1   The Establish E-Mail Address page

9. Click Finish to complete the wizard.

QUESTION   What is the difference between the Sharon S. Salavaria and Chris A. Preston accounts and the Josh Barnhill and Andy Ruth accounts with respect to messaging?

EXERCISE 5.3: CREATING A MAIL-ENABLED DISTRIBUTION GROUP

Estimated completion time: 10 minutes

A mail-enabled distribution group is simply a group of users who will all receive a copy of an e-mail when that e-mail is sent to a specific group address. As many groups within Contoso will need group mail addresses, part of the Contoso Exchange pilot program is showing your team the process by which they can create and populate a mail-enabled distribution group.

> **IMPORTANT**   *Complete the following tasks on Computerxx and Computeryy.*

1. In Active Directory Users And Computers, right-click the Users container, select New, and then click Group.

2. In the New Object – Group dialog box, in the Group Name box, type **Engineersxx** or **Engineersyy**, depending on whether you are using Computerxx or Computeryy.

3. In the Group Type list box, select Distribution, and then click Next.

4. In the New Object – Group dialog box, select the Create An Exchange E-Mail Address check box, review the warning message, and then click Next.

> **QUESTION**   *According to the warning message, what is the best type of distribution group to create and why?*

5. Click Finish to complete the task of creating the new distribution group.

6. Add users to each distribution group as indicated by the following table.

Engineersxx	Engineersyy
Jay Adams, John Arthur, Michael Alexander, Sharon S. Salavaria	Adam Barr, Bryan Baker, Dan Bacon, Chris A. Preston

7. Open Internet Explorer. Click OK to the Internet Explorer Enhanced Security Configuration Message. If using Computerxx, open Outlook Web Access using Sharon Salavaria's credentials; if using Computeryy, open Outlook Web Access using Chris Preston's credentials.

8. Select New. In the To field, enter **Engineersxx** or **Engineersyy**, depending on if you are using Computerxx or Computeryy.

9. In the Subject field, enter **Test message to group**.

10. Click Send.

11. Close and restart Internet Explorer. If using Computerxx, log in using m.alexander's credentials. If using Computeryy, log in using d.bacon's credentials. The password will be P@ssw0rd.

12. Verify that the test message to the group has arrived.

EXERCISE 5.4: DELETING AND RECONNECTING MAILBOXES

Estimated completion time: 15 minutes

As part of the Contoso Exchange pilot program, you wish to run your team members through the process by which they can delete a user's mailbox without deleting his or her user account. You also wish to show them how they can reconnect a deleted mailbox to a specific account if the need arises.

> **IMPORTANT**   Complete the following tasks on Computerxx and Computeryy.

1. In Active Directory Users And Computers, locate and right-click the user you created earlier (Sharon S. Salavaria or Chris A. Preston), and then select Exchange Tasks.

2. In the Exchange Task Wizard, on the Welcome To The Exchange Task Wizard page, click Next.

3. On the Available Tasks page, click Delete Mailbox, and then click Next.

4. On the Delete Mailbox page, shown in Figure 5-2, click Next.

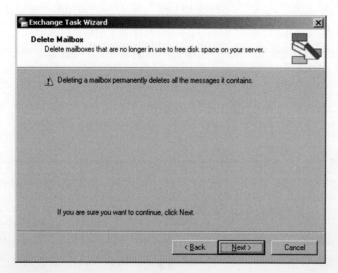

Figure 5-2   Deleting a mailbox

5. Click Finish to complete the wizard.

6. Open Internet Explorer. If using Computer*xx*, navigate to the page *http://localhost/exchange/s.salavaria* entering credentials as appropriate. If using Computer*yy*, navigate to the page *http://localhost/exchange/c.preston* entering credentials as appropriate.

> **QUESTION** What happens when you attempt to navigate to this page and why?

7. Close Internet Explorer.

> **QUESTION** What is the primary difference between deleting the Sharon S. Salavaria and Chris A. Preston accounts, rather than just deleting their associated mailbox?

8. In Exchange System Manager, in the console tree, browse to Administrative Groups/First Administrative Group/Servers/*YourServer*/First Storage Group/Mailbox Store (*YourServer*), and then click Mailboxes.

9. In the console tree, right-click Mailboxes, and select Run Cleanup Agent. Wait until the mailbox for the user listed displays a red X, as shown in Figure 5-3. This might take a few minutes.

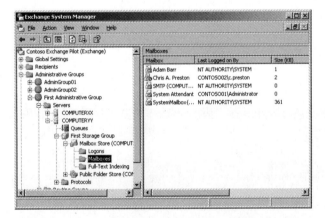

Figure 5-3   The results of running the cleanup agent

10. In the details pane, right-click your user from the preceding table, and then select Reconnect.

11. In the Select A New User For This Mailbox dialog box, type the username that corresponds to the deleted mailbox, and then click OK.

12. Click OK when you are notified that the operation completed successfully.

13. Log off, and then log back in.

14. To verify that the mailbox is reconnected, open Internet Explorer. If using Computerxx, navigate to the page *http://localhost/exchange/ s.salavaria* entering credentials as appropriate. If using Computeryy, navigate to the page *http://localhost/exchange/c.preston* entering credentials as appropriate.

> **QUESTION** If you had actually deleted the Sharon S. Salavaria or Chris A. Preston accounts earlier, would you have been able to reconnect their mailboxes?

EXERCISE 5.5: CONFIGURING STORAGE LIMITS ON INDIVIDUAL MAILBOXES

Estimated completion time: 10 minutes

As a part of the Contoso Exchange pilot program, you want to test setting mailbox limits on individual mailboxes to determine the optimal settings for Contoso when Exchange Server 2003 is finally rolled out. Two of your pilot program users have volunteered to let you use their mailboxes to help you determine the best settings. You will use Active Directory Users And Computers to configure storage limits on those individual mailboxes.

> **IMPORTANT** Complete the following tasks on Computerxx and Computeryy.

1. In Active Directory Users And Computers, in the details pane of the Users container, right-click Sharon Salavaria's user account if you are using Computerxx or Chris Preston's user account if you are using Computeryy, and then select Properties.

2. In the Properties dialog box, click the Exchange General tab.

3. On the Exchange General tab, click Storage Limits.

4. In the Storage Limits dialog box, in the Storage Limits area, clear the Use Mailbox Store Defaults check box.

5. In Storage Limits area, select the Issue Warning At (KB) check box, and then type **10**.

6. Select the Prohibit Send At (KB) check box, and then type **40000**.

7. Select the Prohibit Send And Receive At (KB) check box, and then type **50000**.

8. In the Deleted Item Retention area, clear the Use Mailbox Store Defaults check box.

9. In the Keep Deleted Items For (Days) text box, type **30**.

10. Select the Do Not Permanently Delete Items Until The Store Has Been Backed Up check box, and then click OK.

11. In the Properties dialog box, click OK.

EXERCISE 5.6: CREATING A QUERY-BASED DISTRIBUTION GROUP

Estimated completion time: 10 minutes

You want the members of the Contoso Exchange pilot program team to have the knowledge to create dynamic query-based distribution groups. This will allow them to configure mail groups based on any of the properties of a user's account.

> **IMPORTANT**   Complete the following tasks on Computerxx and Computeryy.

1. Open Active Directory Users And Computers, and edit the following user accounts, setting their Office on the General tab of the account Properties dialog box as specified in the following table.

	Computerxx	**Computeryy**
User Accounts to Edit	Jay Adams, John Arthur	Dan Bacon, Adam Barr
Set Office to	Melbourne	Moscow

2. In Active Directory Users And Computers, right-click the Users container, select New, and then click Query-Based Distribution Group.

3. In the New Object – Query-Based Distribution Group dialog box, in the Query-Based Distribution Group Name box, set the group name to Melbourne_Office for Computerxx and Moscow_Office for Computeryy, and then click Next.

4. Click Customize Filter, and then click Customize.

5. In the Find Exchange Recipients dialog box, click the Advanced tab.

6. In the Find Exchange Recipients dialog box, in the In box, select Entire Directory.

7. On the Advanced tab, click Field, select User, and then click Office Location.

8. On the Advanced tab, in the Condition box, select Is (Exactly). In the Value box, type **Melbourne** for Computerxx and **Moscow** for Computeryy. Click Add, and then click Find Now.

9. Verify that several users are found, and then click OK.

10. In the New Object – Query-Based Distribution Group dialog box, click Next, and then click Finish.

> **QUESTION** You created a distribution group that will include members from anywhere in Active Directory. How would you configure the group differently if you wanted to limit the membership to a particular organizational unit (OU)?

EXERCISE 5.7: CREATING A NEW STORAGE GROUP AND MAILBOX STORE

Estimated completion time: 10 minutes

The primary purpose for creating separate storage groups is if one set of users has a completely different set of backup requirements than another. You will simulate this for the Contoso Exchange pilot program by creating a separate storage area for your company's executives. The actual process of backing up and restoring the storage group is dealt with during a later phase of the pilot program.

> **IMPORTANT** Complete the following tasks on Computerxx and Computeryy.

1. In Exchange System Manager, in the console tree, expand Administrative Groups\First Administrative Group\Servers, right-click either Computerxx or Computeryy depending on which computer you are using, select New, and then click Storage Group.

2. In the Properties dialog box, in the Name text box, type **Executive SG**, and then click OK.

3. In the console tree, right-click Executive SG, select New, and then click Mailbox Store.

4. In the Properties dialog box, in the Name text box, type **Executive Mailbox Store**, and click OK.

5. When prompted, click Yes to mount the store, and then click OK.

6. In the console tree, verify that your server now contains the Executive SG storage group and that the Executive SG storage group contains the Executive Mailbox Store.

> **QUESTION** You just created a new storage group to contain the Executive Mailbox Store. What reason is there for placing this new mailbox store in a new storage group, rather than in the default storage group?

EXERCISE 5.8: MOVING A STORAGE GROUP

Estimated completion time: 10 minutes

As part of the Contoso Exchange pilot program, you want your team to have experience moving storage groups from one location on the storage media to another. This might become necessary, for example, if a new set of disk drives is added and you wish to take advantage of their increased speed and reliability.

> **IMPORTANT** Complete the following tasks on Computerxx and Computeryy.

1. In Exchange System Manager, expand the Administrative Groups\First Administrative Group\Servers node, then expand either Computerxx or Computeryy depending on which computer you are using, right-click Executive SG, and then select Properties.

2. In the Executive SG Properties dialog box, on the General tab, next to the Transaction Log Location box, click Browse.

3. In the Transaction Log dialog box, in the Folders list, select the Exchsrvr folder, click Make New Folder, type **Execs** for the folder name, and press ENTER.

4. In the Transaction Log dialog box, in the Folders list, select the Execs folder, and then click OK.

5. In the Executive SG Properties dialog box, click OK.

6. In the Exchange System Manager dialog box, click Yes to confirm that you want to change the location for the transaction log files and that to do so, any stores in the storage group will be temporarily dismounted.

7. In the Executive SG dialog box, click OK to confirm that the paths have been successfully changed.

QUESTION   What impact does moving a storage group have on the user?

EXERCISE 5.9: CREATING AN OFFLINE ADDRESS LIST

Estimated completion time: 10 minutes

When the Contoso Exchange rollout is completed, you want your users to be able to download a copy of the GAL that they can use when working remotely. A survey of your users has found that users mostly communicate with other users on the same Exchange server. You have decided that you will reduce the amount of information that your users download only to users who are on the same Exchange server rather than every user in the entire Contoso organization. For the Exchange pilot program, you will use Exchange System Manager to create an offline address list that can be associated with a mailbox store.

IMPORTANT   Complete the following tasks on Computerxx and Computeryy.

1. In Exchange System Manager, in the console tree, expand the Recipients container.

2. In the console tree, right-click Offline Address Lists, select New, and then click Offline Address List.

3. In the New Object – Offline Address List dialog box, in the Offline Address List Name text box, type **All_Users_Computerxx** or **All_Users_Computeryy**, and then click Browse.

4. In the Select Exchange Server dialog box, in the Enter The Object Name To Select text box, type **Computerxx** or **Computeryy**, and then click OK.

5. In the New Object – Offline Address List dialog box, click Next.

6. In the next New Object – Offline Address List dialog box, click Add.

7. In the Select Address Lists dialog box, type **All Users**, and then click OK.

8. In the New Object – Offline Address List dialog box, click Default Global Address List, click Remove, and then click Next.

9. Read the warning that indicates that this new offline address list will not be available to clients until the store maintenance period is complete. If you have not changed your store maintenance schedule, the maintenance occurs daily between 1:00 A.M. and 5:00 A.M. Then click Next.

10. Click Finish to finish the task of creating the offline address list.

11. In the console tree, click Offline Address Lists. In the details pane, verify that the offline address list exists.

> **QUESTION**   In step 9, you are warned that the offline address list will not be available until your store maintenance period is complete. How can you force the store maintenance to complete earlier? What would be the impact of forcing store maintenance to complete earlier?

EXERCISE 5.10: CREATING A NEW RECIPIENT POLICY

Estimated completion time: 10 minutes

You want to be able to demonstrate to the Exchange pilot team members how they can apply settings on the mailboxes of your general user population to limit how long they can save e-mail messages. Contoso's legal department is currently working on developing a mail retention policy, and once it is finalized you will want to put it into effect. You will use Exchange System Manager to create a new recipient policy that will limit how long general users can save e-mail messages in their mailboxes.

> **IMPORTANT**   Complete the following tasks on Computerxx and Computeryy.

1. In Exchange System Manager, in the console tree, expand Recipients.

2. Right-click Recipient Policies, select New, and then click Recipient Policy.

3. In the New Policy dialog box, select the Mailbox Manager Settings check box, and then click OK.

4. In the Properties dialog box, on the General tab, in the Name text box, type **Computerxx** (or **Computeryy**) **Mailbox Policy**, as shown in Figure 5-4, and then click Modify.

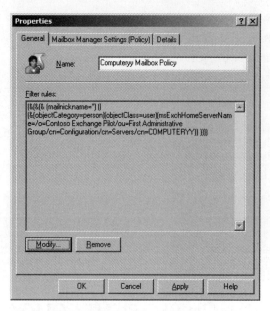

Figure 5-4   Configuring a recipient policy

5. In the Find Exchange Recipients dialog box, on the General tab, in the Show These Recipients area, clear all options except Users With Exchange Mailbox.

6. Select the Storage tab, click Mailboxes On This Server, and then click Browse.

7. In the Select Exchange Server dialog box, type either **Computer*xx*** or **Computer*yy***, and then click OK.

8. In the Find Exchange Recipients dialog box, click Find Now, and then click OK.

9. Read the Exchange System Manager warning regarding policies that are applied to existing users, and then click OK.

10. In the Properties dialog box, click the Mailbox Manager Settings (Policy) tab. In the When Processing A Mailbox list, select Delete Immediately.

11. In the Folder list, for the Inbox folder, click 30, and then click Edit.

12. In the Folder Retention Settings dialog box, in the Age Limit (Days) text box, type **1**, clear the Message Size (KB) check box, and then click OK.

13. In the Properties dialog box, on the Mailbox Manager Settings (Policy) tab, select the Send Notification Mail To User After Processing check box, and then click Message.

14. Verify that the default message is appropriate, select the Insert The Number Of Messages Processed check box, and then click OK.

15. In the Properties dialog box, click OK to create the policy.

16. In the Recipient Policies container, in the details pane, right-click the newly created policy, and select Apply This Policy Now.

17. In the Exchange System Manager dialog box, click Yes.

QUESTION   *Describe what the policy you just created does.*

REVIEW QUESTIONS

Estimated completion time: 20 minutes

1. In your own words, describe what you learned during this lab.

2. Why did you need to initialize a new mailbox?

3. You deleted a mailbox and then reconnected it to a user account. If you deleted the user instead of deleting the mailbox, what steps would you need to complete to reconnect the mailbox?

4. You configured storage limits on an individual mailbox. What would be a better way of applying those same settings to a group of mailboxes? How would this be better?

5. When you moved the transaction log files, you moved them to another folder on the same hard disk as the database files. If you had multiple physical disks, what would have been a better choice for moving the files?

LAB CHALLENGE 5.1: MOVING A DATABASE STORE

Estimated completion time: 20 minutes

You will move the database files for the Executive Mailbox Store to the C:\Exch-srvr\Execs folder. You will then take a screen shot showing the new location for the database store files and submit it to your instructor.

LAB CHALLENGE 5.2: CHANGING A MAIL RETENTION POLICY

Estimated completion time: 20 minutes

Change the mail retention policy so that all items in a user's Inbox and Sent Items folders are deleted after 45 days. Take a screen shot of the Mailbox Manager Settings (Policy) tab showing these settings in effect.

LAB 6
PUBLIC FOLDERS

This lab contains the following exercises and activities:

- Exercise 6.1: Preparation Tasks

- Exercise 6.2: Creating Public Folders Using Outlook Web Access

- Exercise 6.3: Creating Public Folders Using Exchange System Manager

- Exercise 6.4: Creating a General-Purpose Public Folder Tree and an Associated Store

- Exercise 6.5: Mail-Enabling a Public Folder

- Exercise 6.6: Enabling the Security Tab on All Exchange Server Objects

- Exercise 6.7: Granting and Verifying Permissions to Create a Top-Level Folder

- Exercise 6.8: Configuring and Verifying Permissions to Access Public Folders

- Exercise 6.9: Replicating Public Folders

- Review Questions

- Lab Challenge 6.1: Creating a Public Store Policy

- Lab Challenge 6.2: Modifying a Public Store Policy

SCENARIO

Part of the Contoso, Ltd. Microsoft Exchange Server 2003 deployment plan is to use public folders to improve communications between Contoso's disparate departments and sites. With this in mind, you will be examining several aspects of public folder management as a part of the Contoso Exchange pilot program. Specifically you will look at methods of public folder creation and replication. In addition you will configure security to limit access to public folders to select groups of Contoso employees.

After completing this lab, you will be able to:

- Create public folders using Microsoft Outlook Web Access and Exchange System Manager.
- Create new general-purpose public folder trees.
- Mail-enable public folders.
- Manage security settings on public folder trees and public folders.
- Replicate public folders between Exchange servers.
- Configure public store policies to manage storage limits, public folder aging, and public folder replication.

Estimated lesson time: 110 minutes

BEFORE YOU BEGIN

To successfully complete this lab, you will need the following:

- Two networked computers with Microsoft Windows Server 2003 installed using the stand-alone configuration according to the setup guide.
- Windows Server 2003 CD.
- Exchange Server 2003 Enterprise Edition CD.
- To have completed all exercises and lab challenges in Labs 1, 2, 3, and 5. If you have performed Lab 4, ensure that all exercises and lab challenges have been completed.

> **NOTE**   This lab is written to be performed on two computers. If each student has only a single computer, students can work as partners and share computers when needed. The first computer will be Computerxx, and the second computer will be Computeryy. Computerxx typically has an odd-numbered name, such as Computer01 and Computer03. Computeryy typically has an even-numbered name, such as Computer02 and Computer04. If you are unsure of your computer's name, run a command prompt and run the hostname command to find out. Unless otherwise specified, all user accounts used in this lab use the password P@ssw0rd.

EXERCISE 6.1: PREPARATION TASKS

Estimated completion time: 10 minutes

For the public folders phase of the Contoso Exchange pilot program you need to create several user accounts. Each of these user accounts is used in certain aspects of the program and represents a different scenario you wish to test prior to the actual rollout itself.

> **IMPORTANT** *Complete the following tasks on Computerxx and Computeryy.*

1. Log on with the Administrator account.

2. If using Computerxx, create the following users: Eric Lang (e.lang), Jon Ganio (j.ganio), and FolderAdminxx. If using Computeryy, create the following users: Christie Moon (c.moon), Ben Smith (b.smith), and FolderAdminyy. Set each user's password to P@ssw0rd, and ensure that the Password Never Expires check box is selected. Allow a mailbox to be created for each user on his or her respective computer in the First Storage Group/Mailbox Store.

3. On Computerxx, add user FolderAdminxx to the Contosoxx Exchange.Admins group. On Computeryy, add user FolderAdminyy to the Contosoyy Exchange.Admins group.

> **QUESTION** *What effect does adding the FolderAdmin user to the Exchange.Admins group have and why? How else could you achieve a similar result?*

4. Close Active Directory Users And Computers.

EXERCISE 6.2: CREATING PUBLIC FOLDERS USING OUTLOOK WEB ACCESS

Estimated completion time: 10 minutes

Eventually each Contoso site will have a shared repository for general company e-mail messages specific to that location. In this part of the Contoso Exchange pilot program, your team will use Outlook Web Access to create a public folder for your location. The interesting thing about this procedure is that it does not rely upon using Exchange System Manager as a tool. Instead, you will use Outlook Web Access.

> **IMPORTANT** *Complete the following tasks on Computerxx and Computeryy.*

1. Open Outlook Web Access by starting Microsoft Internet Explorer. Click OK to any Internet Explorer Enhanced Security Configuration messages.

2. Enter the URL *http://localhost/exchange/*. If using Computer*xx*, enter the credentials for the FolderAdmin*xx* user. If using Computer*yy*, enter the credentials for the FolderAdmin*yy* user.

3. In the Outlook Web Access window, on the Navigation pane, click Public Folders.

> **NOTE**   *You might need to reauthenticate. You might also need to add the site to your trusted sites list.*

4. In the Public Folders window, in the public folders tree, right-click Public Folders, and then select New Folder.

5. In the Create New Folder dialog box, shown in Figure 6-1, in the Name text box, type **Melbourne** if you are using Computer*xx* or **Moscow** if you are using Computer*yy*, and then click OK.

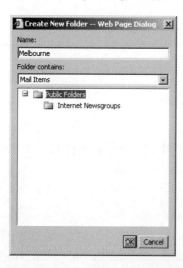

Figure 6-1   Creating a new public folder using Outlook Web Access

6. In the public folders tree, verify that the folder you just created exists.

7. Close the Public Folders windows.

EXERCISE 6.3: CREATING PUBLIC FOLDERS USING EXCHANGE SYSTEM MANAGER

Estimated completion time: 10 minutes

Each department at Contoso requires a shared repository for departmental communication and document sharing. You will use Exchange System Manager to create a public folder for each department.

> **IMPORTANT**   *Complete the following tasks on Computerxx and Computeryy.*

1. Open Exchange System Manager.

2. In Exchange System Manager, in the console tree, browse to the Administrative Groups\First Administrative Group\Folders container, and then expand Folders.

3. In the console tree, right-click Public Folders, select New, and then click Public Folder.

4. If using Computerxx, in the Properties dialog box, in the Name text box, type **Research**, and then click OK. If using Computeryy, in the Properties dialog box, in the Name text box, type **Development**, and then click OK.

5. Right-click the Administrative Groups\First Administrative Group\Folders\Public Folders node, and select Send Hierarchy. Ensure that all check boxes are selected and that changes replicated in the last day are transmitted (see Figure 6-2).

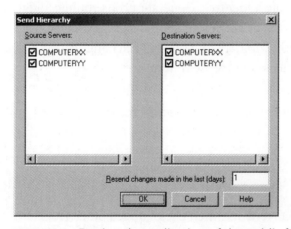

Figure 6-2   Forcing the replication of the public folder hierarchy.

6. Expand the Public Folders node, and then verify that the folder you created using Outlook Web Access and the folder you created using Exchange System Manager exist.

> **NOTE** It might take a few minutes for the public folder hierarchy to replicate to both servers.

7. Open Outlook Web Access using your computer's FolderAdmin account.

8. In the Outlook Web Access window, on the button bar, click Public Folders.

9. Verify that the Melbourne, Moscow, Research and Development public folders are listed.

10. Close the Public Folders window.

EXERCISE 6.4: CREATING A GENERAL-PURPOSE PUBLIC FOLDER TREE AND AN ASSOCIATED STORE

Estimated completion time: 10 minutes

Whereas the Default (or MAPI client) public folder tree exists on every public folder server, general-purpose public folder trees exist only on the server on which they were configured. Once Exchange Server 2003 is rolled out across Contoso's worldwide network, general-purpose public folder trees will be used to extend public folders to some of Contoso's business partners. As you cannot perform this task using Outlook Web Access, you will use Exchange System Manager to create a general-purpose public folder tree. General-purpose public folder trees must be associated with a specific public folder store. You also will use Exchange System Manager to create a public folder store on your Exchange server and associate the general-purpose public folder tree with that store.

> **IMPORTANT** Complete the following tasks on Computerxx and Computeryy.

1. Open Exchange System Manager and in the console tree, browse to Administrative Groups\First Administrative Group\Folders.

2. Right-click Folders, select New, and then click Public Folder Tree.

3. In the Properties dialog box, in the Name text box, type the public folder tree name listed in the following table, and then click OK.

	Computerxx	**Computeryy**
Public Folder Tree	Engineering Tree	Marketing Tree
Public Store	Engineering Public Store	Marketing Public Store

4. Verify that the public folder tree you created exists in the Folders container.

5. In Exchange System Manager, in the console tree, expand Servers, and then expand Computerxx or Computeryy (depending on which one you are using).

6. Right-click First Storage Group, select New, and then click Public Store.

7. In the Properties dialog box, in the Name text box, type the public store name listed in the preceding table, and then click Browse.

8. In the Select A Public Folder Tree dialog box, select the corresponding public folder tree listed in the preceding table, and then click OK.

9. In the Properties dialog box, shown in Figure 6-3, click OK.

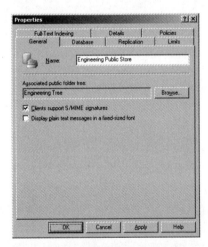

Figure 6-3 Associating a public store with a public folder tree

10. Click Yes when prompted to mount the store.

11. Click OK to acknowledge that the store was successfully mounted.

12. In Exchange System Manager, in the console tree, expand First Storage Group, and then verify that the public folder store that you created (Engineering Public Store or Marketing Public Store) exists.

> **QUESTION** You just created the Engineering Tree on Computerxx and the Marketing Tree on Computeryy. If you had additional public folder servers in the same routing group as well as in other routing groups, on what other public folder servers will this new tree exist?

EXERCISE 6.5: MAIL-ENABLING A PUBLIC FOLDER

Estimated completion time: 10 minutes

As part of the Exchange rollout you will be allowing users to select a public folder from the Global Address List (GAL) when sending departmental e-mail messages. This will provide a convenient centralized archive of all important departmental communications. To simulate this for the Contoso Exchange pilot program, you will use Exchange System Manager to mail-enable a public folder so users can send e-mail to the folder instead of posting to it. Your team will verify this using Outlook Web Access.

> **IMPORTANT**   *Complete the following tasks on Computerxx and Computeryy.*

1. In Exchange System Manager, in the console tree, browse to the Folders\Public Folders container, and then expand the Public Folders container.

2. If using Computerxx, right-click the Research public folder. If using Computeryy, right-click the Development public folder. Then select All Tasks, and then click Mail Enable.

3. Open Internet Explorer and log into Outlook Web Access using your computer's FolderAdmin account.

4. In the Outlook Web Access window, on the toolbar, click New.

5. In the Untitled Message box, in the To text box, type the public folder name, and then on the toolbar click Check Names as shown in Figure 6-4.

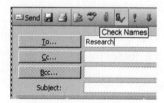

Figure 6-4   The check names icon

6. If prompted, add the Web site to the Trusted Sites zone.

7. In the Subject text box, type **Mail-Enabled Public Folder Test**, and then click Send.

8. In the Outlook Web Access window, on the button bar, click Public Folders.

9. In the Public Folders window, select the public folder listed in the pre-ceding table, and verify that the message you sent now appears in the details pane for that folder.

10. Close the Public Folders window, and then log off Outlook Web Access.

EXERCISE 6.6: ENABLING THE SECURITY TAB ON ALL EXCHANGE SERVER OBJECTS

Estimated completion time: 10 minutes

By default, not all Exchange Server objects display the Security tab when you view them with the object's Properties dialog box. You will enable the Security tab for all Exchange server objects using the Registry Editor.

> **IMPORTANT** *Complete the following tasks on Computerxx and Computeryy.*

1. Click Start, select Run, in the Open box type **regedit**, and then press ENTER.

2. In the Registry Editor dialog box, browse to HKEY_CURRENT_USER\Software\Microsoft\Exchange.

3. Right-click EXAdmin, select New, and then click DWORD Value.

4. In the New Value #1 box, as shown in Figure 6-5, type **ShowSecurityPage**, and then press ENTER.

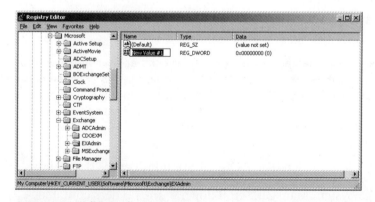

Figure 6-5 Editing the registry

5. In the details pane, double-click ShowSecurityPage, and in the Edit DWORD Value dialog box, in the Value Data text box, type **1**, and then click OK.

6. Close Registry Editor.

EXERCISE 6.7: GRANTING AND VERIFYING PERMISSIONS TO CREATE A TOP-LEVEL FOLDER

Estimated completion time: 15 minutes

Although it is intended that the Contoso public folder structure is easy to navigate for the user community, you do not want the day-to-day creation of public folders to be dependent on the IT staff alone. You will delegate the responsibility of creating departmental public folders to the administrative assistant for each department. To simulate this for the pilot program, you will configure your Exchange Server 2003 organization so that dummy accounts representing departmental administrative assistants have permission to create top-level folders.

> **IMPORTANT**   Complete the following tasks on Computerxx and Computeryy.

1. Switch to Exchange System Manager. In the console tree, right-click Contoso Exchange Pilot (Exchange), and then select Properties.

2. In the Properties dialog box, click the Security tab.

3. On the Security tab, click Add.

4. If using Computerxx, type **Eric Lang**. If using Computeryy, type **Christie Moon**. Click Check Names, and then click OK.

5. On the Security tab, in the Group Or User Names box, select the user you entered in step 4, and then, in the Permissions For section, clear all check boxes except for Create Top Level Public Folder and Special Permissions. Do not modify Special Permissions, as it is supposed to remain unavailable.

> **NOTE**   Note that some check boxes will not appear as cleared until you clear subsequent check boxes. If you are having permissions troubles, ensure that the Administrator account is a member of the exchange.full.admins group and that group is delegated the Exchange Full Administrator role.

6. Click OK to close the Exchange Organization Properties dialog box.

7. In Exchange System Manager, scroll down to the Folders container, right-click Public Folders, and then click Properties.

8. On the Security tab, verify that the user entered in step 4 is configured to allow the Create Top Level Public Folder permission.

9. Click Cancel to close the Public Folders Properties dialog box.

> **QUESTION**   You granted Eric Lang and Christie Moon permission to create top-level public folders. By default, who is allowed to create top-level public folders?

10. Open Internet Explorer and navigate to *http://localhost/exchange*. If using Computer*xx*, log on as j.ganio. If using Computer*yy*, log on as b.smith.

11. In the Outlook Web Access window, on the button bar, click Public Folders.

12. In the Public Folders window, in the public folders tree, right-click Public Folders, and then click New Folder.

13. If using Computer*xx*, set the public folder name to **Purchasing**. If using Computer*yy*, set the public folder name to **Sales**. Click OK.

> **QUESTION**   Were you able to create the public folder? Why?

14. Click OK to close the Microsoft Internet Explorer error dialog box.

15. Click Cancel to close the Create New Folder dialog box.

16. Close all windows and restart Internet Explorer. Navigate to *http://localhost/exchange*.

17. If using Computer*xx*, log in as e.lang. If using Computer*yy*, log in as c.moon.

18. Repeat steps 12 and 13.

19. In the public folders tree, verify that the public folder you just created exists.

20. Close the Public Folders window, and then log off Outlook Web Access.

EXERCISE 6.8: CONFIGURING AND VERIFYING PERMISSIONS TO ACCESS PUBLIC FOLDERS

Estimated completion time: 15 minutes

When your team rolls out Exchange across the Contoso organization, you want to be sure that only a specific set of users will be able to create new items in a public folder. At the same time, you want to be sure that all users can read items that are in a public folder, as these folders will serve as important departmental information archives. In pursuit of these goals, the Contoso Exchange pilot team will use Exchange System Manager to configure default access permissions for a folder in the Default public folder tree.

IMPORTANT   *Complete the following tasks on Computerxx and Computeryy.*

1. Switch to Exchange System Manager, and then browse to Folders\Public Folders.

2. If using Computerxx, right-click the Purchasing public folder. If using Computeryy, right-click the Sales public folder. Select Properties.

NOTE   *If you do not see the folder, you might need to refresh the view of the Public Folders container.*

3. In the Properties dialog box, click Permissions.

4. On the Permissions tab, click Client Permissions.

5. In the Client Permissions dialog box, verify that Default is selected, and then, in the Roles box, select Reviewer.

QUESTION   *What is the meaning of the Default permission?*

6. In the Client Permissions dialog box, select Anonymous, click Remove, and then click OK.

7. In the Properties dialog box, click OK.

8. Open Outlook Web Access using Internet Explorer. If using Computerxx, log on as j.ganio. If using Computeryy, log on as b.smith.

9. In the Outlook Web Access window, on the button bar, click Public Folders.

10. If using Computerxx, click the Purchasing public folder. If using Computeryy, click the Sales public folder.

11. In the details pane, click New to create a new post in the folder.

QUESTION   *Were you able to create a post in the public folder? Why?*

12. Close the HTTP 403 (Forbidden) – Microsoft Internet Explorer window.

13. Close all windows, and restart Internet Explorer. Navigate to *http:// localhost/exchange*.

14. If using Computer*xx*, log in as e.lang. If using Computer*yy*, log in as c.moon.

15. Repeat steps 9, 10, and 11.

16. In the Subject text box, type **Post Test**, and then click Post.

> **QUESTION** Were you able to create a post in the public folder? Why?

17. Close the Public Folders window, and then close Outlook Web Access.

EXERCISE 6.9: REPLICATING PUBLIC FOLDERS

Estimated completion time: 10 minutes

When a public folder is created in the Default public folder tree, the folder name is replicated to all public folder servers in the Exchange Server 2003 organization. It is important to realize that the content of the public folder resides only on the server where the public folder was created. This has implications for those that need to access public folder content over long and slow wide area network (WAN) links, such as those that connect each of Contoso's sites around the world. Public folder replication allows for creating copies of the content of a public folder on other Exchange servers in the Exchange Server 2003 organization. In this exercise the Contoso Exchange pilot team will simulate the replication of public folder information from one server to another so that a similar process can be easily implemented once the global rollout of Exchange begins.

> **IMPORTANT** Complete the following tasks on Computer*xx* and Computer*yy*.

1. Switch to Exchange System Manager, browse to Folders\Public Folders, and then expand Public Folders.

2. If using Computer*xx*, right-click the Research public folder. If using Computer*yy*, right-click the Development public folder. Select Properties.

3. In the Properties dialog box, click Replication.

4. On the Replication tab, click Add.

5. In the Select A Public Store dialog box, verify that your partner's server is selected, and then click OK.

6. In the Properties dialog box, click OK.

7. Expand the Public Folders node.

8. If using Computerxx, select the Research public folder. If using Computeryy, select the Development public folder.

9. In the details pane, click the Replication tab, and then verify that both Computerxx and Computeryy are listed.

> **QUESTION**   If Computerxx and Computeryy were connected through a slow WAN link and the link was becoming overloaded, what could you do to ensure that Exchange Server delivered user-generated messages before the public folder replication messages?

10. If using Computerxx, right-click the Research public folder. If using Computeryy, right-click the Development public folder. Select All Tasks, and then click Send Contents.

11. In the Send Contents dialog box, in the Source Servers list, select the check box next to your server.

12. In the Send Contents dialog box, in the Destination Servers list, select the check box next to your partner's server.

13. In the Send Contents dialog box, in the Resend Changes Made In The Last (Days) text box, type **1**, and then click OK.

14. In the Exchange System Manager dialog box, click Yes to confirm that sending changes can cause a large volume of network traffic.

REVIEW QUESTIONS

Estimated completion time: 15 minutes

1. In your own words, describe what you learned during this lab.

2. Why did you need to create a new public folder store for the general-purpose public folder tree?

3. Why would you want to control who can create top-level public folders?

4. What actions can a user with the Reviewer role perform on a public folder?

5. Why would you want to replicate public folders?

6. What is the best way to control public folder limits and replication settings on individual public folder stores instead of on individual public folders?

7. You need to configure a public folder so that it is excluded from the storage limits policy applied to the public folder store. What should you do?

LAB CHALLENGE 6.1: CREATING A PUBLIC STORE POLICY

Estimated completion time: 15 minutes

You wish to control the size of public folders so that you can make some type of reliable estimate in terms of budgeting for server storage. Create a system policy container on Computerxx to allow both Computerxx and Computeryy to create public store policy.

On both computers, create a public store policy that will:

- Be named Public Store Policy *YourServer*.

- Issue a warning message when the public folder reaches 50,000 KB in size.

- Limit items placed in the public folder to 5,000 KB in size.

- Retain deleted items for 10 days.

- Set a maximum age for any public folder in the public folder store to 1095 days (three years).

Apply the policy that you created to the Default public folder store on your server.

In Exchange System Manager, take a screen shot [CTRL + PRNT SCRN] of the policy settings. Take a screen shot [CTRL + PRNT SCRN] showing the policy is applied to your Default public folder store on your server. Turn both screen shots in to your instructor at the end of the lab.

LAB CHALLENGE 6.2: MODIFYING A PUBLIC STORE POLICY

Estimated completion time: 10 minutes

You wish to add replication settings to the existing public store policies. You will modify the Properties dialog boxes of the existing public store policy, Public Store Policy *YourServer*, to include the Replication tab. You will then configure replication so that it occurs Sunday through Saturday, between midnight and 6 A.M.

In Exchange System Manager, take a screen shot [CTRL + PRNT SCRN] of the policy settings to turn in at the end of the lab.

LAB 7
VIRTUAL SERVERS

This lab contains the following exercises and activities:

- Exercise 7.1: Starting and Verifying the Default POP3 Virtual Server

- Exercise 7.2: Starting and Verifying the Default IMAP4 Virtual Server

- Exercise 7.3: Installing an Enterprise Root Certificate Authority

- Exercise 7.4: Configuring SSL-Only Connections for the POP3 Virtual Server

- Exercise 7.5: Configuring SSL-Only Connections for the IMAP4 Virtual Server

- Review Questions

- Lab Challenge 7.1: Configuring SSL Connections to Outlook Web Access and Resolving Certificate Issues

SCENARIO

This phase of the Contoso Exchange pilot program will focus on allowing clients other than Microsoft Outlook Web Access to retrieve mail from Microsoft Exchange Server 2003. Several of Contoso, Ltd.'s international branch offices are multiplatform environments. Non-Windows clients use e-mail software that only supports the Post Office Protocol version 3 (POP3) protocol. All Windows clients have Microsoft Office Outlook 2003 installed and will be utilizing Internet Message Access Protocol version 4 (IMAP4) because of its increased functionality.

This seventh phase of the Contoso Exchange pilot program begins with the configuration and activation of the appropriate default virtual servers. Once these virtual servers are verified as working, you will configure them to be more secure by requiring Secure Sockets Layer (SSL)-only connections. SSL certificates will be acquired from an internal certificate authority (CA) trusted by all computers within the Contoso forest.

After completing this lab, you will be able to:

- Configure and test the default POP3 virtual server.
- Configure and test the default IMAP4 virtual server.
- Install an enterprise root CA.
- Request and install a SSL certificate on the default POP3 virtual server.
- Request and install a SSL certificate on the default IMAP4 virtual server.
- Force clients of the default POP3 virtual server to use only SSL connections.
- Force clients of the default IMAP4 virtual server to use only SSL connections.

Estimated lesson time: 90 minutes

BEFORE YOU BEGIN

To successfully complete this lab, you will need the following:

- Two networked computers with Microsoft Windows Server 2003 installed, using stand-alone configuration according to the setup guide.
- Windows Server 2003 CD.
- Exchange Server 2003 Enterprise Edition CD.
- To have completed all exercises and lab challenges in Labs 1, 2, 3, 5, and 6. If you have performed Lab 4, ensure that all exercises and lab challenges have been completed.

> **IMPORTANT**   This lab is written to be performed on two computers. If each student has only a single computer, students can work as partners and share computers when needed. The first computer will be Computerxx and the second computer will be Computeryy. Computerxx typically has an odd-numbered name, such as Computer01 and Computer03. Computeryy typically has an even-numbered name, such as Computer02 and Computer04. If you are unsure of your computer's name, at a command prompt run the hostname command. Unless otherwise specified, all user accounts used in this lab use the password P@ssw0rd.

EXERCISE 7.1: STARTING AND VERIFYING THE DEFAULT POP3 VIRTUAL SERVER

Estimated completion time: 10 minutes

POP3 will be used by those employees at Contoso who do not use Windows operating systems. As these employees are scattered across Contoso's many international sites, it is important that your team understand how to configure Exchange Server 2003 to support POP3 clients. In this stage of the Contoso Exchange pilot program you will configure, activate, and test the default POP3 virtual server.

> **IMPORTANT** Complete the following tasks on Computerxx and Computeryy.

1. Log on with the Administrator account.

2. From the Administrative Tools menu, open the services console.

3. Locate the Microsoft Exchange POP3 service.

4. Right-click the Microsoft Exchange POP3 service and select Properties.

5. In the Startup Type drop-down list, select Automatic and click Apply.

6. Click the Start button, shown in Figure 7-1, to start the service.

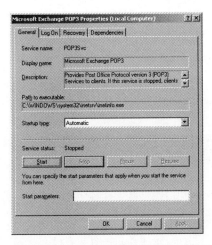

Figure 7-1 Starting the Microsoft Exchange POP3 service

7. Click OK to close the Properties dialog box.

8. From the All Programs menu, open Outlook Express. In the Connection Wizard, in the Display Name text box, enter **Contoso Exchange Pilot** and click Next.

9. If using Computer*xx*, set the e-mail address to **s.salavaria@con-tosoxx.com**. If using Computer*yy*, set the e-mail address to **c.pre-ston@contosoxx.com**.

10. In the My Incoming Mail Server text box, type **POP3**. Set incoming and outgoing mail servers to **localhost**.

11. On the Internet Mail Logon page, leave the default settings and enter the password as **P@ssw0rd**. Click Next. On the final page, click Finish.

12. On the toolbar, click Send/Recv.

13. Click the Inbox to view the message.

> **QUESTION** What messages do you see and when were they sent?

14. Close all open windows.

EXERCISE 7.2: STARTING AND VERIFYING THE DEFAULT IMAP4 VIRTUAL SERVER

Estimated completion time: 10 minutes

As IMAP4 has a greater feature set than POP3, it will be the e-mail protocol of choice at Contoso, Ltd. All Contoso employees who have computers running a Windows operating system will use IMAP4. As this represents the vast majority of users at Contoso, it is important that your team understand how to configure Exchange Server 2003 to support IMAP clients. In this stage of the Contoso Exchange pilot program you will configure, activate, and test the default IMAP4 virtual server.

> **IMPORTANT** Complete the following tasks on Computer*xx* and Computer*yy*.

1. From the Administrative Tools menu, open the Services console.

2. Locate the Microsoft Exchange IMAP4 service.

3. Right-click the Microsoft Exchange IMAP4 service and select Properties.

4. In the Startup Type drop-down list, select Automatic and click Apply.

5. Click Start to start the service.

6. When the service has started, click OK to close the Properties dialog box.

7. Open Microsoft Outlook Express.

8. From the Tools menu, select Accounts.

9. Click Add, and then select Mail.

10. Leave the default setting on the Your Name page and click Next.

11. If using Computer*xx*, set the e-mail address to **e.lang@con-tosoxx.com**. If using Computer*yy*, set the e-mail address to **c.moon@contosoxx.com**. Click Next.

12. In the My Incoming Mail Server type **IMAP**. Set incoming and outgoing servers to **localhost** as shown in Figure 7-2. Click Next.

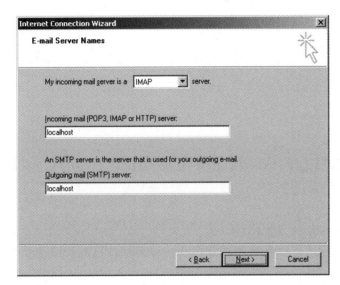

Figure 7-2 Configuring E-mail Server Names

13. On the Internet Mail Logon page, enter the password **P@ssw0rd** and click Next.

14. Click Finish and then click Close.

15. When asked if you would like to download folders, click Yes.

16. In the Show/Hide IMAP folders dialog box, shown in Figure 7-3, select all available public folders except Internet Newsgroups and click Show. Click OK.

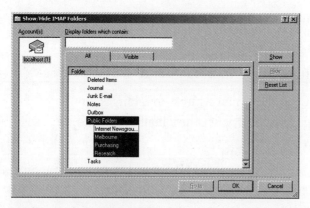

Figure 7-3   Selecting public folders to download in Outlook Express

> **QUESTION**   In which public folders are you able to create a new subfolder named Test?

17. Close all open windows.

EXERCISE 7.3: INSTALLING AN ENTERPRISE ROOT CERTIFICATE AUTHORITY

Estimated completion time: 10 minutes

When Exchange Server 2003 is deployed at the conclusion of the pilot program, you will want to protect the e-mail retrieval process by encrypting the transaction between clients and server using SSL. This requires the installation of a SSL certificate. Although it is possible to acquire a SSL certificate from a third-party provider, at the present time use of certificates from an enterprise root CA will adequately serve the needs of the Contoso Exchange pilot program. You have decided to install a single enterprise root CA on the first pilot program computer. As the second computer is located within the same Active Directory forest, it will automatically trust certificates issued by the first without needing any extra configuration.

> **IMPORTANT**   Complete the following tasks on Computerxx.

1. Log on with the Administrator account.

2. From Control Panel, select Add/Remove Programs and then select Add/Remove Windows Components.

3. Select the Certificate Services check box. A dialog box appears. Read the message, click Yes, and then click Next.

QUESTION After installing Certificate Services, which changes will you be unable to make?

4. On the CA Type page, select Enterprise Root CA and then click Next

QUESTION What is the primary difference between an enterprise root CA and a stand-alone root CA?

5. On the CA Identifying Information page, shown in Figure 7-4, in the Common Name For This CA text box, type **Computerxx**. Click Next.

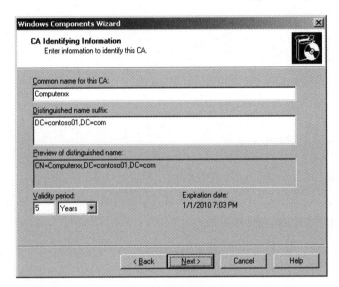

Figure 7-4   CA Identifying Information page

6. Accept the defaults on the Certificate Database Settings page and click Next.

7. Click Yes when presented with the message informing you that Certificate Services must temporarily stop Internet Information Services.

NOTE You might be prompted to enter the Windows Server 2003 Enterprise Edition Evaluation CD at this point. Do so, and click OK.

8. Click Finish when it is presented and close all open windows.

9. From the Start menu, select Run and type **MMC**.

10. From the File menu, add the Certificate Templates snap-in, shown in Figure 7-5, to the console.

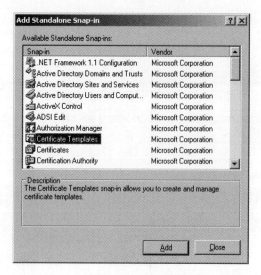

Figure 7-5 Adding the Certificate Templates Snap-in

11. Edit the Properties dialog box of the Web Server certificate template. On the Security tab, add the Contosoyy\Domain Admins group. Click Check Names and then click OK.

12. Ensure that the Contosoyy\Domain Admins group has Read, Write, and Enroll permissions as shown in Figure 7-6. Click OK.

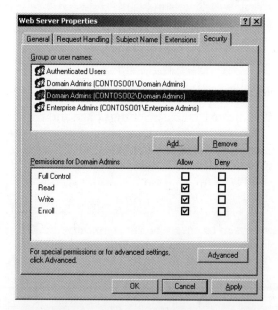

Figure 7-6 Configuring certificate permissions for the domain administrator group in the child domain

13. Close all windows.

IMPORTANT *Complete the following tasks on Computeryy.*

14. Restart Computeryy.

> **NOTE** Restarting Computeryy will allow it to update and learn that there is now an Enterprise Root CA available within the forest.

EXERCISE 7.4: CONFIGURING SSL-ONLY CONNECTIONS FOR THE POP3 VIRTUAL SERVER

Estimated completion time: 15 minutes

Now that the pilot program's enterprise root CA has been installed and configured, you can modify the properties of the default POP3 virtual service to require that communications between client and server are encrypted using SSL. Doing so requires using the Certificate Request Wizard, which can be accessed through the default POP3 virtual service's Properties dialog box. This requests and installs the necessary certificate.

> **IMPORTANT** Complete the following tasks on Computerxx and Computeryy.

1. Open Exchange System Manager, and navigate to the Administrative Groups, First Administrative Group, Servers, Computerxx (or Computeryy), Protocols node.

2. Open the POP3 node, right-click Default POP3 Virtual Server, and select Properties.

3. Click the Access tab. In the Secure Communication box, click Certificate.

4. This starts the Web Server Certificate Wizard. Click Next.

5. Select Create A New Certificate and click Next.

6. Select Send The Request Immediately To An Online Certification Authority. Click Next.

7. Leave the default Certificate Name setting in place and click Next.

8. Set the organization to Contoso Exchange Pilot Program and the organizational unit to Computerxx (or Computeryy) and click Next.

9. Set the common name to Computerxx (or Computeryy) and click Next.

10. Enter your geographical information and click Next.

11. On the Choose A Certification Authority page, in the Certification Authorities drop-down list box, select Computerxx. Click Next.

12. Review the summary information and click Next.

13. Click Finish.

14. From the Start menu, select Run and type **MMC**.

15. Add the Certificates Snap-in, and when asked what the snap-in will manage certificates for, select Computer account for the local computer.

16. In the Personal, Certificates folder, verify that a certificate has been issued with the friendly name Default POP3 Virtual Server.

> **NOTE**   If the certificate has not been issued, verify that the Contosoyy\Domain Admins group has the correct permissions for the Web Server certificate template that you configured in steps 11 and 12 of Exercise 7.3.

17. Close the custom Certificates console and return to the Default POP3 Virtual Server Properties.

18. On the Access tab of the Default POP3 Virtual Server Properties dialog box, click Communication.

19. Select Require Secure Channel and click OK.

20. Click OK to close the Default POP3 Virtual Server Properties dialog box.

21. From the Services console, restart the Microsoft Exchange POP3 Service.

> **NOTE**   In Exchange System Manager, check that the Default POP3 Virtual Server has properly started. If it has not, right-click the object and select start.

22. Start Outlook Express. Close the Error box.

23. From the Tools menu, select Accounts. Click the Mail tab. Edit the first localhost mail account by selecting it and clicking the Properties button. Click the Advanced tab.

> **NOTE**   If there is a field labeled "Incoming Mail (IMAP4)" rather than "Incoming Mail (POP3)" on this tab, you are editing the incorrect mail account.

24. Under Incoming Mail (POP3), select the This Server Requires A Secure Connection (SSL) check box and then click OK. Click Close to close the Internet Accounts dialog box.

25. Click Send/Recv.

26. You will receive a message saying that the certificate's CN name does not match the passed value. Click Yes to continue using this server.

27. Verify that you can check mail.

> **QUESTION**   What could you do to resolve the message mentioned in step 26?

EXERCISE 7.5: CONFIGURING SSL ONLY CONNECTIONS FOR THE IMAP4 VIRTUAL SERVER

Estimated completion time: 15 minutes

In the last exercise, you configured POP3 communication between the client and the server to be encrypted using SSL. In this aspect of the pilot program you will follow a similar procedure to force IMAP4 communications between the client and the server to be encrypted using SSL. You will then test that the change has been implemented correctly by attempting to access the IMAP4 virtual server insecurely and then securely.

> **IMPORTANT**   Complete the following tasks on Computerxx and Computeryy.

1. Navigate to the Administrative Groups, First Administrative Group, Servers, Computerxx (or Computeryy), Protocols, IMAP4 node of Exchange System Manager.

2. Right-click the Default IMAP4 Virtual Server and select Properties.

3. On the Access tab, click Certificate.

4. Repeat steps 4 through 13 from Exercise 7.4, but change the default certificate name from IMAP4 to POP3.

5. On the Access tab of the Default IMAP4 Virtual Server Properties dialog box, click Communication.

6. Select Require Secure Channel and click OK.

7. Click OK to close the Default IMAP4 Virtual Server Properties dialog box.

8. From the Services console, restart the Microsoft Exchange IMAP4 Service.

> **NOTE** In Exchange System Manager, check that the Default POP3 Virtual Server has properly started. If it has not, right-click the object and select start.

9. Start Outlook Express. Close the Error box.

> **QUESTION** What happened when you started Outlook Express this time?

10. From the Tools menu, select Accounts.

11. Click the Mail tab. Edit the second localhost mail account by selecting it and clicking the Properties button. Click the Advanced tab.

> **NOTE** If there is a field labeled "Incoming Mail (POP3)" rather than "Incoming Mail (IMAP4)" on this tab, you are editing the incorrect mail account.

12. Under Incoming Mail (IMAP4), select the This Server Requires A Secure Connection (SSL) check box and then click OK. Click Close to close the Internet Accounts dialog box.

13. You will be asked if you would like to refresh your folder list. Click Yes.

14. Verify that you can check mail.

REVIEW QUESTIONS

Estimated completion time: 20 minutes

1. In your own words, describe what you learned during this lab.

2. What are the main differences between the POP3 and IMAP4 protocols?

3. Which ports do POP3-SSL and IMAP4-SSL use?

4. Other than requesting a new certificate for the IMAP4 virtual server from a CA, what other method could you use to ensure that IMAP4 client connections use SSL?

5. Why did you need to alter the permissions of the Certificate template in step 11 of Exercise 7.3?

LAB CHALLENGE 7.1: CONFIGURING SSL CONNECTIONS TO OUTLOOK WEB ACCESS AND RESOLVING CERTIFICATE ISSUES

Estimated completion time: 40 minutes

Part of the pilot program involves assessing the knowledge that you have gained to this point. That includes performing small tasks for which you do not have full instructions, but which you should be able to complete by using the knowledge you have gained during these exercises.

> **IMPORTANT**   *Complete the following tasks on Computerxx and Computeryy.*

- Configure the POP3 and IMAP4 account settings in Outlook Express so that you no longer receive the message that the certificate's CN does not match the passed value. Take a screen shot of the settings that you changed to resolve this problem and submit it to your instructor.

- Restrict access to Microsoft Outlook Web Access to SSL connections only. Take a screen shot of the correctly configured Secure Communications dialog box.

LAB 8
SMTP PROTOCOL CONFIGURATION AND MANAGEMENT

This lab contains the following exercises and activities:

■ Exercise 8.1: Configuring DNS to Support SMTP

■ Exercise 8.2: Configuring the SMTP Server to Require Authentication

■ Exercise 8.3: Configuring the Default SMTP Virtual Server to Only Accept SSL Connections

■ Exercise 8.4: Configuring Default SMTP Virtual Server Properties

■ Exercise 8.5: Creating and Configuring an SMTP Connector

■ Review Questions

■ Lab Challenge 8.1: Reconfiguring SMTP Settings for IMAP4 Accounts

■ Lab Challenge 8.2: Creating an Additional Virtual SMTP Server

SCENARIO

In this stage of the Contoso Exchange pilot program you will be configuring the default Simple Mail Transfer Protocol (SMTP) virtual server. The default SMTP virtual server is responsible for receiving e-mail sent from clients such as Microsoft Outlook 2003 and Microsoft Outlook Express, as well as for receiving incoming e-mail from remote SMTP servers such as those on the Internet.

After completing this lab, you will be able to:

■ **Create Mail Exchanger (MX) records in Domain Name System (DNS).**

■ **Configure the default virtual SMTP server to require authentication.**

■ **Configure the default virtual SMTP server to only accept Secure Sockets Layer (SSL) connections.**

■ Configure virtual SMTP server properties.

■ Create and configure an SMTP Connector.

Estimated lesson time: 90 minutes

BEFORE YOU BEGIN

To successfully complete this lab, you will need the following:

■ Two networked computers with Microsoft Windows Server 2003 installed using stand-alone configuration according to the setup guide

■ Windows Server 2003 CD

■ Exchange Server 2003 Enterprise Edition CD

■ To have completed all exercises and lab challenges in Labs 1, 2, 3, 4, 5, 6, and 7

> **IMPORTANT**   This lab is written to be performed on two computers. If each student has only a single computer, students can work as partners and share computers when needed. The first computer will be Computerxx and the second computer will be Computeryy. Computerxx typically has an odd-numbered name, such as Computer01 and Computer03. Computeryy typically has an even-numbered name, such as Computer02 and Computer04. If you are unsure of your computer's name, at a command prompt, run the hostname command to find out. Unless otherwise specified, all user accounts used in this lab use the password P@ssw0rd.

EXERCISE 8.1: CONFIGURING DNS TO SUPPORT SMTP

Estimated completion time: 10 minutes

Remote SMTP servers use MX records to locate partner SMTP servers when they need to transfer mail. MX records are special DNS records that point to existing host records in the DNS zone. It is usually prudent to have several MX records within a zone. In the event that the primary SMTP server fails, mail will then be routed to another SMTP server that has been assigned a lower priority.

> **IMPORTANT**   Complete the following tasks on Computerxx.

1. Log on with the Administrator account.

2. In Active Directory Users and Computers, check that the Contosoyy\Administrator account is a member of the Enterprise Admins group. If not, add this account to this group and close the console.

3. From the Administrative Tools menu, open the DNS console.

4. Expand the Computer*xx*, Forward Lookup Zones, Contoso*xx*.com node.

5. Right-click the Contoso*xx*.com node and select New Mail Exchanger (MX).

6. Click Browse and double-click Computer*xx*, then double-click Forward Lookup Zones, and then Contoso*xx*.com.

7. Select the Computer*xx* record as shown in Figure 8-1 and then click OK.

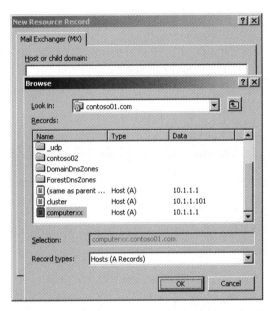

Figure 8-1   Selecting a target Host (A record) for an MX record.

8. Set the Mail Server Priority to 20 and click OK.

> **IMPORTANT**   *Complete the following tasks on Computeryy.*

9. Open a command prompt. Type the command **dnscmd computer*xx* / recordadd contoso*xx*.com computer*yy* A *X.X.X.X*** (where *X.X.X.X* is the IP address of Computer*yy*).

> **NOTE**   *You should receive a message stating that the A record for Computeryy was successfully added to the Contosoxx.com zone. If not, ensure that you have carried out step 2 corectly.*

10. Type the command **dnscmd computerxx /recordadd contosoxx.com computeryy MX 10 computeryy.contosoxx.com**. You will receive a similar message to the one you received after step 9.

> **QUESTION** *Which of the two mail records will have priority for the Contosoxx.com zone?*

EXERCISE 8.2: CONFIGURING THE SMTP SERVER TO REQUIRE AUTHENTICATION

Estimated completion time: 15 minutes

Authentication can be configured on the default SMTP virtual server to ensure that only authorized personnel can use that server to send e-mail. As this can add another layer of security to your organization's messaging infrastructure, you are investigating it as a part of the Contoso Exchange pilot program.

> **IMPORTANT** *Complete the following tasks on Computerxx and Computeryy.*

1. Open Exchange System Manager and navigate to the Administrative Groups, First Administrative Group, Servers, Computerxx (or Computeryy), Protocols, SMTP node.

2. Right-click the default SMTP virtual server and select Properties.

3. On the Access tab, click Authentication.

4. Clear the Anonymous Access and Basic Authentication check boxes, as shown in Figure 8-2, and click OK.

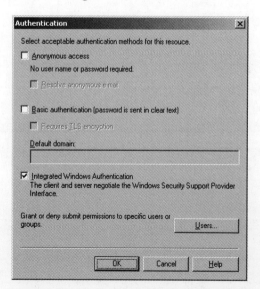

Figure 8-2 Configuring SMTP virtual server authentication options

5. Click OK to close the Default SMTP Virtual Server Properties dialog box.

6. Open Outlook Express.

7. Click the Create Mail icon. If using Computer*xx*, address the e-mail to **s.salavaria@contoso*xx*.com**. If using Computer*yy*, address the e-mail to **c.preston@contoso*xx*.com**. In the Subject field, enter **SMTP Test** and click Send.

> **QUESTION**   What message did you receive when you attempted to send the e-mail?

8. Close the error window.

9. From the Tools menu, select Accounts. Click the Mail tab and edit the localhost account by clicking the Properties button.

10. On the Servers tab, select the My Server Requires Authentication check box. Click Settings.

11. Select Log On Using. If using Computer*xx*, in the Account Name text box type **s.salavaria**, and in the Password text box type **P@ssw0rd**. If using Computer*yy*, in the Account Name text box enter **c.preston**, and in the Password text box type **P@ssw0rd**. Click OK and then click OK again to close the Account Properties dialog box.

12. Click Close to exit the Internet Accounts dialog box.

13. Repeat step 7.

> **NOTE**   Both the original message and this one will now be transmitted to the SMTP server.

EXERCISE 8.3: CONFIGURING THE DEFAULT SMTP VIRTUAL SERVER TO ONLY ACCEPT SSL CONNECTIONS

Estimated completion time: 15 minutes

One of the business managers, after hearing about how his IMAP4 mail could be encrypted using SSL, wants you to test how mail being transmitted to a mail server could be protected in the same manner. In this phase of the Contoso Exchange pilot program you will configure the default SMTP virtual server to only accept SMTP traffic encrypted using an SSL certificate.

IMPORTANT   *Complete the following tasks on Computerxx and Computeryy.*

1. Open Exchange System Manager and in the console tree browse to Administrative Groups, First Administrative Group, Servers, Computer*xx* (or Computer*yy*), Protocols, SMTP.

2. Right-click the default SMTP virtual server and select Properties.

3. On the Access tab, click Certificate.

4. This starts the Web Server Certificate Wizard. Click Next.

5. Select Create A New Certificate and click Next.

6. Select Send The Request Immediately To An Online Certification Authority. Click Next.

7. Leave the default Certificate Name setting in place and click Next.

8. Set the organization to Contoso Exchange Pilot Program and the organizational unit to Computer*xx* (or Computer*yy*).

9. Set the common name to Computer*xx* (or Computer*yy*).

10. Enter your Geographical Information and click Next.

11. On the Choose A Certification Authority page, in the Certification Authorities drop-down list box, select Computer*xx*. Click Next.

12. Review the summary information and click Next.

13. You will be informed that a certificate is now installed on this server. Click Finish.

14. Click Communication.

15. On the Security page, select the Require Secure Channel check box and click OK.

16. Click OK to close the Default SMTP Virtual Server Properties dialog box.

17. Open Outlook Express.

18. Click the Create Mail icon. If using Computer*xx*, address the e-mail to **s.salavaria@contoso*xx*.com**. If using Computer*yy*, address the e-mail to **c.preston@contoso*xx*.com**. In the Subject field, enter **SMTP SSL Test** and click Send.

QUESTION   *What message did you receive when you attempted to send the e-mail?*

19. Close the Error dialog box.

20. From the Tools menu, select Accounts. Click the Mail tab.

21. Select the Localhost account and click the Properties button.

22. On the Advanced tab, under Outgoing Mail (SMTP), select the This Server Requires A Secure Connection (SSL) check box as shown in Figure 8-3. Click OK.

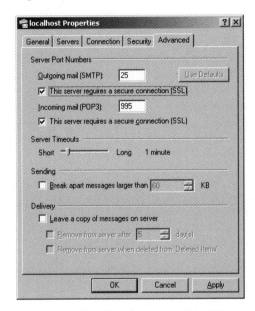

Figure 8-3   Configuring outgoing SSL support for Outlook Express

23. Click Close to close the Internet Accounts dialog box.

24. Repeat step 18.

EXERCISE 8.4: CONFIGURING DEFAULT SMTP VIRTUAL SERVER PROPERTIES

Estimated completion time: 15 minutes

Another part of the Contoso Exchange pilot program is configuring the SMTP server to accept only a limited number of connections at any one time and to only forward message traffic of a reasonable size. Many of Contoso's international sites have slow Internet connections and failure to impose these limits can mean that the link gets bogged down when a single user attempts to send an attachment that is too large.

> **IMPORTANT**   Complete the following tasks on Computerxx and Computeryy.

1. Open Exchange System Manager and in the console tree browse to Administrative Groups, First Administrative Group, Servers, Computer*xx* (or Computer*yy*), Protocols, SMTP.

2. Right-click the default SMTP virtual server and select Properties.

3. On the General tab, select the Limit Number Of Connections To check box and enter a value of **10**.

4. On the Access tab, click Relay.

5. In the Relay Restrictions dialog box, click Add. If using Computer*xx*, enter the IP address of Computer*yy*. If using Computer*yy*, enter the IP address of Computer*xx* as shown in Figure 8-4. Click OK.

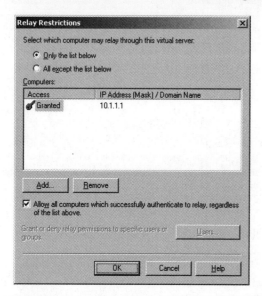

Figure 8-4   Setting relay restrictions of the default virtual SMTP server

6. Click OK to close the Relay Restriction dialog box.

7. On the Messages tab, select the Limit Message Size To (KB) check box and enter **2048**.

8. Select the Limit Session Size To (KB) check box and enter **6144**.

> **QUESTION**   How many sessions would be required to send out 10 different 1.5-megabyte e-mails?

9. On the Delivery tab, click Advanced.

10. Select the Perform Reverse DNS Lookup On Incoming Messages check box. Click OK.

11. Click OK to close the Default SMTP Virtual Server Properties box.

EXERCISE 8.5: CREATING AND CONFIGURING AN SMTP CONNECTOR

Estimated completion time: 15 minutes

Contoso has partners who are connected over virtual private network (VPN) links to the organization's network. You want to create SMTP Connectors to forward e-mail directly to these partner organizations. You also want to explore how to restrict particular users from sending e-mail to these partner organizations.

> **IMPORTANT** *Complete the following tasks on Computerxx and Computeryy.*

1. In Exchange System Manager, navigate to the Administrative Groups, First Administrative Group, Routing Groups, First Routing Group, Connectors node.

2. Right-click the Connectors node and select New SMTP Connector.

3. If using Computerxx, name the connector Connectorxx. If using Computeryy, name the connector Connectoryy.

4. If using Computerxx, add Computeryy as a bridgehead. If using Computeryy, add Computerxx as a bridgehead as shown in Figure 8-5.

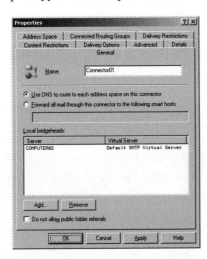

Figure 8-5 Configuring an SMTP Connector

5. On the Address Space tab, click Add.

6. Select the SMTP Address Type and click OK.

7. If using Computerxx, set the e-mail domain to Tailspintoys.com. If using Computeryy, set the e-mail domain to Adatum.com. Click OK.

8. On the Delivery Restrictions tab, under Reject Messages From, click Add.

9. If using Computer*xx*, enter **folderadmin*xx*@contoso*xx*.com**. If using Computer*yy*, enter **folderadmin*yy*@contoso*yy*.contoso*xx*.com**.

10. Click OK to close the SMTP Connector Properties dialog box.

REVIEW QUESTIONS

Estimated completion time: 20 minutes

1. In your own words, describe what you learned during this lab.

2. Describe the benefits of performing a reverse DNS lookup on incoming messages.

3. Why wouldn't you use an enterprise root CA as the source of an SSL certificate for an SMTP virtual server that communicates with other SMTP servers on the Internet?

4. For what reasons would you want to limit the size of individual messages and sessions?

5. How can you allow only certain members of the organization to send e-mail to addresses on the Internet?

LAB CHALLENGE 8.1: RECONFIGURING SMTP SETTINGS FOR IMAP4 ACCOUNTS

Estimated completion time: 15 minutes

Part of the pilot program involves assessing the knowledge that you have gained to this point. That includes performing small tasks for which you do not have full instructions, but which you should be able to complete using the knowledge you have gained during today's exercises. When you originally configured Outlook Express in Lab 7, you did so for both a POP3 account and an IMAP4 account. In this lab you configure the SMTP settings only for the POP3 account. Configure the IMAP4 account so that you are able to do the following:

- Send an e-mail from Computer*xx* using the e.lang account.

- Send an e-mail from Computer*yy* using the c.moon account.

- Take screen shots of the Servers and the Advanced tabs on the IMAP4 account's Properties dialog box and submit them to your lab instructor.

LAB CHALLENGE 8.2: CREATING AN ADDITIONAL VIRTUAL SMTP SERVER

Estimated completion time: 20 minutes

Part of the pilot program involves assessing the knowledge that you have gained to this point. That includes performing small tasks for which you do not have the full instructions, but which you should be able to complete using the knowledge you have gained during today's exercises. You will create a second virtual SMTP server with the following properties.

- On Computer*xx*, this virtual server will be called Server*xx*.

- On Computer*yy*, this virtual server will be called Server*yy*.

- The virtual server will use an SMTP port of 2525.

- The virtual server will use a smart host at mail.contoso*xx*.com.

- Make a screen shot of the new virtual SMTP server functioning alongside the default virtual SMTP server. Make a screen shot of the Advanced Delivery properties dialog box specifying the appropriate smart host.

LAB 9
MICROSOFT EXCHANGE SERVER 2003 SECURITY

This lab contains the following exercises and activities:

- Exercise 9.1: Installing Exchange Server 2003 Service Pack 1

- Exercise 9.2: Enabling Connection Filtering

- Exercise 9.3: Blocking all E-Mail from a Specific E-Mail Address and an Entire Domain

- Exercise 9.4: Creating a New Encryption and Digital Signature Certificate Template for Use by Exchange Users

- Exercise 9.5: Using Digital Signatures and Encryption

- Review Questions

- Lab Challenge 9.1: Blocking Specific Domains from Sending SMTP Traffic to the Default SMTP Virtual Server

- Lab Challenge 9.2: Creating an Advanced Exchange User Certificate Template

SCENARIO

Microsoft Exchange Server 2003 security has many aspects. One aspect is ensuring that your Exchange Server 2003 software is up to date. It is also very important that the platform that hosts Exchange Server 2003, be it Microsoft Windows 2000 or Microsoft Windows Server 2003, also has the most recent security updates installed. Another aspect is creating and updating a list of blocked users and sites that have a history of sending undesirable e-mail to your organization. A third aspect is ensuring that e-mail is only visible to those for whom it is intended, and that there is a reliable method by which the sender's identity can be verified. These three aspects are explored in phase 9 of the Contoso Exchange Server pilot program as your team works through the planned exercises.

After completing this lab, you will be able to:

- Install a Windows Server 2003 hotfix and Exchange Server 2003 Service Pack 1.
- Configure and enable connection filtering.
- Block all e-mail from a specific e-mail address.
- Block all e-mail from a specific domain.
- Create a new digital certificate template for use by Exchange users.
- Obtain an Exchange User certificate for a user.
- Digitally sign and encrypt e-mail using Microsoft Outlook Web Access.

Estimated lesson time: 100 minutes

BEFORE YOU BEGIN

To successfully complete this lab, you will need the following:

- Two networked computers with Windows Server 2003 installed using stand-alone configuration according to the setup guide
- Windows Server 2003 CD
- Exchange Server 2003 Enterprise Edition CD
- Update for Windows Server 2003: KB 831 464 WindowsServer2003-KB831464-x86-ENU.exe
- Exchange Server 2003 Service Pack 1 E3SP1ENG.EXE
- To have completed all exercises and lab challenges in Labs 1 through 8

> **IMPORTANT**   This lab is written to be performed on two computers. If each student has only a single computer, students can work as partners and share computers when needed. The first computer will be Computerxx, and the second computer will be Computeryy. Computerxx typically has an odd-numbered name, such as Computer01 and Computer03. Computeryy typically has an even-numbered name, such as Computer02 and Computer04. If you are unsure of your computer's name, run a command prompt and run the hostname command to find out. Unless otherwise specified, all user accounts used in this lab use the password P@ssw0rd.

EXERCISE 9.1: INSTALLING EXCHANGE SERVER 2003 SERVICE PACK 1

Estimated completion time: 20 minutes

It is important for any administrator to be well practiced in the art of applying hotfixes and service packs. In this stage of the Contoso Exchange pilot program you will apply a Windows Server 2003 hotfix and Exchange Server 2003 Service Pack 1 to the servers that you have been working on.

IMPORTANT *Complete the following tasks on Computerxx and Computeryy.*

1. Log on with the Administrator account.

2. Locate the WindowsServer2003-KB831464-x86-ENU.exe file, and double click it.

3. This launches the Windows Server 2003 KB831464 Setup Wizard. Click Next.

4. Review the license agreement, and select I Agree. Click Next.

   The update then will install.

5. Click Finish to close the wizard.

   NOTE *Your computer may reboot at this point.*

6. Locate the E3SP1ENG.exe file, and double-click it.

7. In the Choose Directory For Extracted Files dialog box enter **c:\sp1**, as shown in Figure 9-1, and click OK.

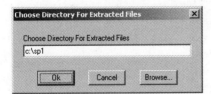

Figure 9-1 Choose a directory for extracted files

8. Open My Computer, and navigate to the C:\Sp1\E3sp1eng\Setup\I386 directory.

9. Double-click the file Update.exe. This starts the Microsoft Exchange 2003 Service Pack Installation Wizard. Click Next.

10. On the License Agreement page, review the license agreement and select I Agree. Click Next.

11. Review the information on the Component Selection page, and then click Next.

12. Review the Installation Summary page, and then click Next.

    Exchange Server 2003 is updated by the Service Pack software. This takes several minutes.

13. When the wizard completes, click Finish.

EXERCISE 9.2: ENABLING CONNECTION FILTERING

Estimated completion time: 15 minutes

Connection filtering allows you to use block lists. Block lists are special lists that list Simple Mail Transfer Protocol (SMTP) servers that are known to have forwarded unsolicited commercial e-mail in the past. Although using block lists can be effective, most senders of unsolicited commercial e-mail shift the IP address and domain name of the servers that they use every time they perform a mail out.

> **IMPORTANT**   Complete the following tasks on Computerxx only.

1. Open Exchange System Manager, and select the Global Settings node.

2. Right-click Message Delivery, and select Properties.

3. On the Connection Filtering tab, shown in Figure 9-2, click Add.

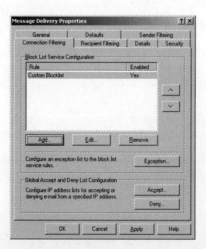

Figure 9-2   Configuring the Connection Filtering tab

4. In the Display Name text box type **Custom Blocklist**. In the DNS Suffix Of Provider text box, type **blocklists.contosoxx.com**. Click OK.

5. Click OK to close the Message Delivery Properties dialog box.

6. You are presented with an informational message. Read it, and then click OK.

> **QUESTION** What does the message inform you about connection filtering?

> **IMPORTANT** Complete the following tasks on Computerxx and Computeryy.

7. In Exchange System Manager, navigate to the Administrative Groups, First Administrative Group, Servers, Computerxx (or Computeryy), Protocols, SMTP node.

8. Right-click Default SMTP Virtual Server, and select Properties.

9. On the General tab, click Advanced.

10. In the Advanced dialog box, click Edit.

11. In the Identification dialog box, select the Apply Connection Filter check box, and then click OK.

12. In the Advanced dialog box, verify that Filter Enabled is set to Yes, and then click OK.

13. Click OK to close the Default SMTP Virtual Server Properties dialog box.

EXERCISE 9.3: BLOCKING ALL E-MAIL FROM A SPECIFIC E-MAIL ADDRESS AND AN ENTIRE DOMAIN

Estimated completion time: 15 minutes

Although it is likely that Contoso will use block lists when Exchange Server 2003 is deployed throughout the organization, you wish to experiment with blocking individual e-mail addresses and SMTP servers from accessing the default virtual SMTP server.

> **IMPORTANT** Complete the following tasks on Computerxx only.

1. Open Exchange System Manager.

2. Navigate to Global Settings.

3. Right-click Message Delivery, and then select Properties.

4. On the Sender Filtering tab, click Add.

5. In the Add Sender dialog box, type **marko.zajc@cpandl.com**, and then click OK.

6. In the Message Delivery Properties dialog box, ensure that the Drop Connection If Address Matches Filter check box is selected, and then click OK.

7. Close the Public Folders window.

8. Acknowledge the informational message by clicking OK.

> **IMPORTANT** *Complete the following tasks on Computerxx and Computeryy.*

9. In Exchange System Manager, navigate to the Administrative Groups, First Administrative Group, Servers, Computerxx (or Computeryy), Protocols, SMTP node.

10. Right-click Default SMTP Virtual Server, and select Properties.

11. In the Default SMTP Virtual Server Properties dialog box, click the Access tab.

12. Click Connection.

13. In the Connection dialog box, ensure that All Except The List Below is selected, and then click Add.

14. In the Computer dialog box, click Domain.

15. Read the SMTP configuration message, and then click OK.

> **QUESTION** *What is the drawback to restricting access by domain name?*

16. In the Domain field, type **treyresearch.com**, and then click OK twice.

17. In the Default SMTP Virtual Server Properties dialog box, click the General tab, and then click Advanced.

18. Click Edit.

19. In the Identification dialog box, select the Apply Sender Filter check box, and then click OK.

20. Click OK to close the Advanced dialog box.

21. Click OK to close the Default SMTP Virtual Server Properties dialog box.

EXERCISE 9.4: CREATING A NEW ENCRYPTION AND DIGITAL SIGNATURE CERTIFICATE TEMPLATE FOR USE BY EXCHANGE USERS

Estimated completion time: 15 minutes

The existing Exchange User certificate template does not meet the needs of Contoso. As part of the Contoso Exchange pilot program you will create and test a new Exchange User certificate template that will allow the use of encryption as well as digital signatures.

IMPORTANT   *Complete the following tasks on Computerxx only.*

1. From the Start menu, select Run, and type **mmc**.

2. Add the Certificate Templates Snap-in to the custom console.

3. Right-click the Exchange User template, and select Duplicate Template.

4. On the General tab of the New Template Properties dialog box, in the Template Display Name text box, type **New Exchange User.**

5. On the Request Handling tab, set the Purpose drop-down list box to Signature And Encryption as shown in Figure 9-3.

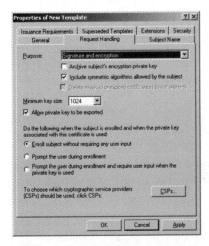

Figure 9-3   Request Handling tab of New Template Properties dialog box

6. On the Superseded Templates tab, click Add, and then select Exchange User Template. Click OK.

7. On the Security tab, configure the Authenticated Users group to have Read, Enroll and Autoenroll (Allow) permissions. Configure the Enterprise Admins group to have Full Control (Allow) permission.

8. Click OK to close the New Template Properties dialog box.

9. From the Administrative Tools menu, open the Certification Authority console.

10. Expand the Computerxx node. Right-click Certificate Templates, and select New Certificate Template.

11. Select the New Exchange User template, and click OK.

EXERCISE 9.5: USING DIGITAL SIGNATURES AND ENCRYPTION

Estimated completion time: 15 minutes

To secure communications within Contoso, you want to be able to verify the sender's identity and also have the message be unreadable to anyone outside the Contoso organization. You will do this by utilizing the encryption and digital signature functionality of Outlook Web Access.

> **IMPORTANT**   Complete the following tasks on Computerxx and Computeryy.

1. From the Start menu, select Search. Locate the file Setupmcl.exe.

2. When the file is found, double-click the file located in the Exchsrvr directory to install it.

> **QUESTION**   What is the location of the other setupmcl.exe file, and how did it get there?

> **NOTE**   This installs an Outlook Web Access Secure Multipurpose Internet Mail Extensions (S/MIME) component on the computer that cannot currently be installed in the normal way because of the secure configuration of the server.

3. If using Computerxx, add user s.salavaria to the Backup Operators group. If using Computeryy, add user c.preston to the Backup Operators group.

4. In Exchange System Manager, edit the properties of the default SMTP virtual Server and allow Anonymous access.

5. Log off.

6. If using Computer*xx*, log back on as s.salavaria. If using Computer*yy*, log back on as c.preston.

7. Open Internet Explorer. Navigate to *https://computerxx/certsrv*.

8. On the Welcome page, click Request A Certificate.

9. If you are using Computer*xx*, select User Certificate, and click Submit. Click Yes when queried about whether you want to request a certificate now. After waiting for the certificate to be generated, click Install This Certificate. In the dialog box that opens, click Yes to indicate that you trust the Web site and want the certificate installed. Go to step 9.

10. If you are using Computer*yy*, select Create And Submit A Request To This CA. On the Advanced Certificate Request page, ensure that New Exchange User is selected. Fill out the information in the form as shown in the following table.

Name	C.Preston
E-Mail	c.preston@contosoxx.com
Company	Contoso
Department	Engineering
City	Melbourne
State	Victoria
Country/Region	AU

11. When finished, click Submit. Click Yes when queried about whether you want to request a certificate now. Click Install This Certificate. In the dialog that opens, click Yes to indicate that you trust the Web site and want the certificate installed.

12. Close Internet Explorer.

13. Open Outlook Express.

14. You will be required to enter e-mail account credentials.

	Computer*xx*	Computer*yy*
Display Name	Sharon Salavaria	Chris Preston
E-mail address	s.salavaria@contosoxx.com	c.preston@contosoxx.com
Incoming Mail Server Type	IMAP	IMAP
Imcoming and outgoing server	computer*xx*	computer*yy*

	Computerxx	Computeryy
Account name	s.salavaria	c.preston
Password	P@ssw0rd	P@ssw0rd

15. Configure the Advanced tab properties of the account to require outgoing SMTP and SSL connections.

16. Click Create Mail.

17. If using Computerxx, address the e-mail to **s.salavaria@contosoxx.com**. If using Computeryy, address the e-mail to **c.preston@contosoxx.com**.

18. In the Subject text box, type **Encryption Test**.

19. On the Tools menu, check the Encrypt and Digitally Sign options.

20. In the body of the message, type **This is a test of encryption**, and then click Send.

21. Click the Send/Recv icon to retrieve the sent e-mail from the mail server.

22. Verify that the e-mail was digitally signed by s.salavaria or c.preston and that the message was encrypted.

23. Close all windows, and log off.

REVIEW QUESTIONS

Estimated completion time: 20 minutes

1. In your own words, describe what you learned during this lab.

2. Why is adding individual e-mail addresses to the block list an inefficient method of controlling unsolicited commercial e-mail?

3. Why should hotfixes and service packs be tested on a limited number of computers instead of being installed on all computers as soon as they are released?

4. In terms of functionality, what is the difference between the existing Exchange User template and the New Exchange User template created in Exercise 9.4?

5. What icons are used in Outlook Web Access to indicate that a message is both encrypted and digitally signed?

LAB CHALLENGE 9.1: BLOCKING SPECIFIC DOMAINS FROM SENDING SMTP TRAFFIC TO THE DEFAULT SMTP VIRTUAL SERVER

Estimated completion time: 10 minutes

Part of the pilot program involves assessing the knowledge that you have gained to this point. That includes performing small tasks for which you do not have full instructions, but which you should be able to complete using the knowledge you have gained during today's exercises.

Configure the default virtual SMTP server to block access for all computers in the adventure-works.com, alpineskihouse.com, cohovineyardandwinery.com, fabrikam.com, litwareinc.com, and proseware.com domains. Take a screen shot verifying that these domains have been blocked.

LAB CHALLENGE 9.2: CREATING AN ADVANCED EXCHANGE USER CERTIFICATE TEMPLATE

Estimated completion time: 20 minutes

Part of the pilot program involves assessing the knowledge that you have gained to this point. That includes performing small tasks for which you do not have the full instructions, but which you should be able to complete using the knowledge you have gained during today's exercises.

You will create a new certificate template to supersede the New Exchange User template. The new template must have the following properties:

- The template will be called Advanced Exchange User Template.

- It will have a validity of 2 years and a renewal period of 12 weeks.

- It will have a minimum key size of 8192.

- It should cause outgoing mail to be signed and encrypted.

- It should prompt the user during enrollment.

- Subject name should be built from Active Directory information.

- The template should supersede the New Exchange User template.

- Take screen shots of the General, Request Handling, and Subject Name tabs of the Certificate Template Properties dialog box.

- This challenge can only be completed on Computer*xx*, as it hosts the Certification Authority.

TROUBLESHOOTING LAB B

SECURE POP3 ACCESS AND MAILBOX PROBLEMS

Troubleshooting Lab B is a practical application of the knowledge you have acquired from Labs 5 through 9. Your instructor or lab assistant has changed your computer configuration, causing it to "break." Your task in this lab is to apply your acquired skills to troubleshoot and resolve the break. A scenario is presented that will lay out the parameters of the break and the conditions that must be met for the scenario to be resolved. This troubleshooting lab has two break scenarios. The first break scenario involves secure Post Office Protocol version 3 (POP3) access, and the second break scenario involves problems with accessing mailboxes.

> **NOTE** **Do Not Proceed with This Lab Until You Receive Guidance from Your Instructor** The break scenario that you will be performing will depend on which computer you are using. The first computer will be Computerxx, and the second computer will be Computeryy. Computerxx typically has an odd-numbered name, such as Computer01 and Computer03. Computeryy typically has an even-numbered name, such as Computer02 and Computer04. If you are unsure of your computer's name, run a command prompt and issue the hostname command. If you are using Computerxx, you will perform Break Scenario 1. If you are using Computeryy, you will perform Break Scenario 2. Your instructor or lab assistant might also have special instructions. Consult with your instructor before proceeding.

BREAK SCENARIO 1

> **IMPORTANT** Perform this break scenario on Computerxx.

All POP3 access at Contoso, Ltd. will occur over Secure Sockets Layer (SSL) encrypted connections. Regular POP3 users who connect to Computerxx have recently been unable to check mail in this method. Specifically, the following situations have occurred:

- User s.salavaria is unable to access the secure POP3 server on Computerxx using Microsoft Outlook Express.

- You have checked the Outlook Express settings (configured in Labs 7 and 9) and verified them to be correct. You should not alter Outlook Express settings in troubleshooting this problem.

As you resolve the problem, fill out the worksheet in the TroubleshootingLabB folder and include the following information:

- Description of the problem

- A list of all steps taken to diagnose the problem, even the ones that did not work

- Description of the exact issue and solution

- A list of the tools and resources you used to help solve this problem

BREAK SCENARIO 2

IMPORTANT   *Perform this break scenario on Computeryy.*

Several users of Computeryy have been unable to access their Internet Message Access Protocol version 4 (IMAP4) e-mail. Specifically, the following situations have occurred:

- c.moon is unable to access his mail through IMAP4.

- Other users of Computeryy, including some who use IMAP4, are able to access their mail normally.

- The Outlook Express settings used by c.moon have been checked and are correct.

As you resolve the problem, fill out the worksheet in the TroubleshootingLabB folder and include the following information:

- Description of the problem

- A list of all steps taken to diagnose the problem, even the ones that did not work

- Description of the exact issue and solution

- A list of the tools and resources you used to help solve this problem

LAB 10
BACKUP AND RESTORE

This lab contains the following exercises and activities:

■ Exercise 10.1: Creating a Recovery Storage Group

■ Exercise 10.2: Enabling the Volume Shadow Copy Service

■ Exercise 10.3: Performing a Full Online Backup of a Storage Group

■ Exercise 10.4: Public Folder Indexes

■ Exercise 10.5: Recovering a Deleted User's Mailbox

■ Exercise 10.6: Recovering a Mailbox Store Using the Recovery Storage Group

■ Exercise 10.7: Merging Recovered Mailbox Data

■ Review Questions

■ Lab Challenge 10.1: Volume Shadow Copies and Restoring the Executive SG

SCENARIO

As any experienced systems administrator knows, restoring lost data from backup can be a stressful task. In this phase of the Contoso Exchange pilot program you will guide your team through the procedures to back up Microsoft Exchange Server 2003 and then safely recover it. You will return to these exercises after the completion of the Contoso Exchange Pilot Program so that your team can gain confidence performing the restoration procedure.

After completing this lab, you will be able to:

■ Create a recovery storage group.

■ Enable the Volume Shadow Copy service on specific volumes.

■ Perform a full online backup of a storage group.

■ Re-create corrupted public folder indexes.

■ Recover a deleted user's mailbox.

■ Recover a mailbox store.

■ Recover user mailbox data from backup.

Estimated lesson time: 100 minutes

BEFORE YOU BEGIN

To successfully complete this lab, you will need the following:

■ Two networked computers with Microsoft Windows Server 2003 installed using stand-alone configuration according to the setup guide

■ Windows Server 2003 CD

■ Exchange Server 2003 Enterprise Edition CD

■ To have completed all Lab Challenges in Labs 1 through 9

> **IMPORTANT**   This lab is written to be performed on two computers. If each student has only a single computer, students can work as partners and share computers when needed. The first computer will be Computerxx, and the second computer will be Computeryy. Computerxx typically has an odd-numbered name, such as Computer01 and Computer03. Computeryy typically has an even-numbered name, such as Computer02 and Computer04. If you are unsure of your computer's name, open a command prompt window and run the hostname command to find out. Unless otherwise specified, all user accounts used in this lab use the password P@ssw0rd.

EXERCISE 10.1: CREATING A RECOVERY STORAGE GROUP

Estimated completion time: 5 minutes

The recovery storage group (RSG) allows data to be restored to an Exchange Server 2003 computer without the need for a separate recovery server. Data to be recovered is shifted from backups to the RSG and from there to the appropriate data storage group. In this phase of the Contoso Exchange pilot program, you will create an RSG. This storage group will be used later in the day to assist you in the recovery of data. Use the following procedure to create the storage group.

> **IMPORTANT**   Complete the following tasks on Computerxx and Computeryy.

1. Log on with the Administrator account.

2. Create the folder C:\Recovery.

3. Open Exchange System Manager.

4. Navigate to the Administrative Groups, First Administrative Group, Servers node.

5. If using Computer*xx*, right-click Computer*xx*. If using Computer*yy*, right-click Computer*yy*. Select New Recovery Storage Group.

6. The Recovery Storage Group Properties dialog box appears as shown in Figure 10-1.

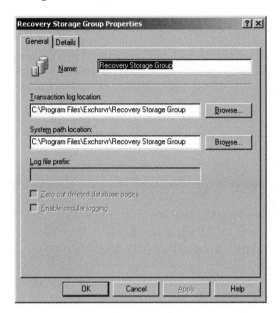

Figure 10-1   Creating a recovery storage group

7. Change the Transaction Log Location and the System Path Location settings to C:\Recovery.

> **QUESTION**   Given these settings, what is the default location for restored mailbox store files?

8. Click OK to create the RSG.

9. From the Administrative Tools Menu, select Internet Information Services (IIS) Manager.

10. Navigate to the Web Sites, and right-click on Default Web Site.

11. Click on the Directory Security tab. In the Secure communications box, click Edit.

12. Remove the check next to Require Secure Channel (SSL), and click OK.

13. Click OK to close the default Web Site Properties.

14. When presented with the Inheritance Overrides dialog, click Select All, and then click OK.

15. Restart the Default Web Site.

EXERCISE 10.2: ENABLING THE VOLUME SHADOW COPY SERVICE

Estimated completion time: 10 minutes

The Volume Shadow Copy service allows point-in-time backups to be taken of open files. Enabling this service on important volumes significantly enhances the capabilities of the Windows Server 2003 Backup utility. To enable this service, use the following procedure.

> **IMPORTANT**   Complete the following tasks on Computerxx and Computeryy.

1. Open My Computer.

2. Right-click Drive C, and select Properties.

3. On the Shadow Copies tab, ensure that volume C:\ is selected, and click Enable.

4. You will be presented with a dialog box. Read the information, and then click Yes.

5. Click Settings.

6. Change the Maximum Size setting to No Limit.

7. In the Settings dialog box, click Schedule.

8. Click Delete twice to remove the currently configured schedules.

9. Click OK to close the Schedule dialog box. Click OK to close the Settings dialog box.

10. Click Create Now as shown in Figure 10-2 to create a shadow copy of the selected volume.

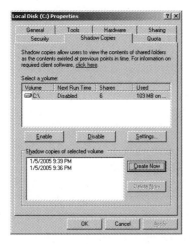

Figure 10-2 Create a shadow copy of the selected volume

11. Verify that a new shadow copy exists.

12. In the Shadow Copies Of Selected Volume box, select the older shadow copy, and then click Delete Now.

13. Click OK to close the disk drive Properties dialog box.

EXERCISE 10.3: PERFORMING A FULL ONLINE BACKUP OF A STORAGE GROUP

Estimated completion time: 15 minutes

Regular backups should be made every day. The techniques used to back up an Exchange Server 2003 storage group differ slightly from those used to back up regular files and folders. In this phase of the Contoso Exchange pilot program you will perform a full online backup of each server's main storage group. To perform this exercise, follow this procedure.

> **IMPORTANT**   *Complete the following tasks on Computerxx and Computeryy.*

1. Open Outlook Web Access.

2. If using Computer*xx*, log in as **e.lang**. If using Computer*yy*, log in as **c.moon**.

3. Create three new messages with the titles message one, message two, and message three. If using Computer*xx*, address them to **e.lang@contosoxx.com**. If using Computer*yy*, address them to **c.moon@contosoxx.com**.

4. Synchronize OWA with the Exchange Server, and verify that the three test messages appear in the Inbox.

5. Close Internet Explorer.

6. Create the directory C:\Backups.

7. Navigate to the directory C:\Program files\Exchsrvr\Mdbdata. Take note of the number of .log files.

8. From the Start menu, select All Programs, Accessories, System Tools, and select Backup. This starts the Backup Or Restore Wizard. Click Next.

9. On the Backup Or Restore page, ensure that Back Up All Files And Settings is selected, and then click Next.

10. On the What To Back Up page, select Let Me Choose What To Back Up, and then click Next.

11. On the Items To Back Up page, in the Items To Back Up box, expand Microsoft Exchange Server, Computerxx (or Computeryy), Microsoft Information Store, and select First Storage Group as shown in Figure 10-3. Click Next.

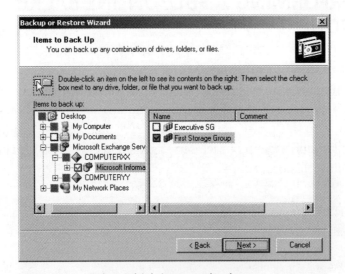

Figure 10-3   Select which items to back up

12. On the Backup Type, Destination, And Name page, click Browse.

13. In the Save As dialog box, browse to C:\Backups. In the File Name text box, type **full_online.bkf**, and then click Save. Click Next.

14. Click Finish to commence the backup.

15. Click Report to check the backup for errors. This opens a text window. Review the information, and then close the window.

16. Click Close to exit the Backup Progress dialog box.

17. Navigate to the directory C:\Program files\Exchsrvr\Mdbdata. Take note of the number of .log files.

> **QUESTION**   What has happened to the number of log files and why?

EXERCISE 10.4: PUBLIC FOLDER INDEXES

Estimated completion time: 15 minutes

In this exercise you create a public folder index, delete it, and then restore it. Unlike other components of Exchange Server 2003, it is impossible to back up a full-text index. Restoring the index requires re-creating it. It is important to note that you can't just click a button to re-create a corrupted index. To perform this exercise, follow this procedure.

> **IMPORTANT**   Complete the following tasks on Computerxx and Computeryy.

1. C:\Program Files\Exchsrvr \ExchangeServer_Server Name\ GatherLogs folder exists. If this folder does not exist, create it.

2. In Exchange System Manager, navigate to Administrative Groups, First Administrative Group, Servers, Computerxx (or Computeryy), First Storage Group.

3. Right-click Public Folder Store, and select Create Full-Text Index.

4. Click OK to accept the default catalog location.

5. Right-click Public Folder Store, and then select Start Full Population.

6. Click Yes to close the warning box and start the update process. Click Yes again to close the subsequent warning box.

7. Expand the Public Folder Store node, and click Full-Text Indexing. It lists a last build time that is today's date. You may have to click Refresh.

> **NOTE**   At this stage, for purposes of this exercise, we assume that you have discovered that the full-text index for this public folder is corrupt. The rest of the exercise deals with how you can remove the corrupt full-text index and the steps that you need to take to replace it.

8. Right-click the Public Folder Store node, and select Delete Full-Text Index. In the dialog box, click Yes to continue.

9. From the Start menu, select Run, type **regedit**, and then click OK.

10. In Registry Editor, navigate to HKEY_LOCAL_MACHINE\ SOFTWARE\Microsoft \Search\1.0\Databases, and then expand Databases.

11. Under Databases, click ExchangeServer_*Server Name*.

12. In the details pane, next to Log Path under Data, locate the folder where the property store and log files are kept. Record the path to this folder because you need it for the next step. By default, the folder is C:\Program Files\Exchsrvr\ExchangeServer_*Server Name*.

13. In Microsoft Windows Explorer, open the folder that you identified in the previous step.

14. In the open folder, verify that the Projects and GatherLogs subfolders are empty. If these folders contain files, delete the files. Do not delete the Projects and GatherLogs folders.

> **NOTE** Depending on the type of corruption that occurred, these folders might have files in them even though they should have been emptied when you attempted to delete the full-text index. As in this exercise the corruption did not really occur, these folders are empty.

15. Close Windows Explorer, and close Registry Editor.

16. Reboot the computer.

17. In Exchange System Manager, right-click Public Folder Store, and then select Create Full-Text Index.

18. In the Public Folder Store (*Server Name*) dialog box, click OK to accept the default location for the catalog.

19. In Exchange System Manager, right-click Public Folder Store (*Server Name*), select Start Full Population, click Yes to continue, and then click Yes again to close the subsequent warning box.

20. Right-click Public Folder Store (*Server Name*), and then select Properties.

21. In the Public Folder Store (*Server Name*) Properties dialog box, click the Full-Text Indexing tab.

22. On the Full-Text Indexing tab, select the This Index Is Currently Available For Searching By Clients check box, click OK, and then click OK again to acknowledge the warning.

> **QUESTION** According to the warning, what should you do prior to making a full-text index available?

23. Close Exchange System Manager.

EXERCISE 10.5: RECOVERING A DELETED USER'S MAILBOX

Estimated completion time: 15 minutes

When you delete a user account using Active Directory Users And Computers, you also delete that user's mailbox. There might be occasions when in the normal course of events, you delete a user account and then later find that you need to recover information from that deleted user's mailbox. In this phase of the Contoso Exchange pilot program you will simulate the recovery of an important message from a deleted user's mailbox.

> **IMPORTANT** Complete the following tasks on Computerxx and Computeryy.

1. If using Computerxx, open Microsoft Outlook Web Access (OWA) by navigating to the page *http://computerxx/exchange*. If using Computeryy, open OWA by navigating to the page *http://computeryy/exchange*.

2. If using Computerxx, log in as s.salavaria. If using Computeryy, log in as c.preston.

3. Click on Options. Remove the check next to Encrypt Contents And Attachments For Outgoing Messages, and remove the check next to Add A Digital Signature To Outgoing Messages. Click Save and Close.

4. Create a new e-mail. In the Subject text box, type **Great Business Contact!** In the body of the e-mail, type **Call 555-1234, Mick wants to buy 100,000 units!** If using Computerxx, address the e-mail to **j.ganio@contosoxx.com**. If using Computeryy, address the e-mail to **b.smith@contosoxx.com**. Click Send to send the e-mail.

5. Close Outlook Web Access.

NOTE   At this stage in the hypothetical scenario, we are going to pretend that the users to whom the important e-mail was sent have left the company. Contoso, Ltd. policy dictates that when a user leaves the company, his or her account is deleted.

6. Open Active Directory Users And Computers. If using Computer*xx*, delete the user account of Jon Ganio. If using Computer*yy*, delete the user account of Ben Smith. Ensure that the Mark Each Selected Exchange Mailbox For Deletion check box is selected, and click Yes.

NOTE   At this point in the hypothetical scenario, it is discovered that there is important business information in the deleted user's mailbox, and that mailbox needs to be recovered.

7. Create a new user named mail_recovery_user. Assign a password of P@ssw0rd. Do not create an Exchange mailbox for this user.

8. Close Active Directory Users And Computers.

9. Open Exchange System Manager. Navigate to the Administrative Groups, First Administrative Group, Servers, Computer*xx* (or Computer*yy*), First Storage Group, Mailbox Store node. Right-click Mailboxes, and select Run Cleanup Agent.

10. You should see a red X icon next to the mailbox of the user that you have just deleted, as shown in Figure 10-4.

Mailbox	Last Logged on By	Size (KB)
Adam Barr	NT AUTHORITY\SYSTEM	1
Ben Smith	S-1-5-21-2332489194-26226...	2
Chris A. Preston	NT AUTHORITY\SYSTEM	3
Christie Moon	CONTOSO02\c.moon	21
FolderAdmin02	CONTOSO02\FolderAdmin02	1
SMTP (COMPUT...	NT AUTHORITY\SYSTEM	0
System Attendant	NT AUTHORITY\SYSTEM	0
SystemMailbox{...	NT AUTHORITY\SYSTEM	361

Figure 10-4   Locating the disconnected mailbox.

11. Right-click the mailbox with the red X icon next to it, and select Reconnect.

12. In the Select A New User For This Mailbox dialog box, enter the user name **mail_recovery_user**. Click OK twice.

13. Open Active Directory Users And Computers and view the properties of the mail_recovery_user account. Verify that the user has access to OWA as shown in Figure 10-5.

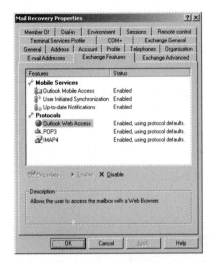

Figure 10-5   Verifying that the mail_recovery_user can access Outlook Web Access

14. Log off, and then log back on.

15. If using Computerxx, open Outlook Web Access by navigating to *http://computerxx/exchange*. If using Computeryy, open Outlook Web Access by navigating to *http://computeryy/exchange*.

16. Log in as mail_recovery_user.

> **NOTE**   It might take several attempts to log in as mail_recovery_user. If you fail to log in several times, restart Microsoft Internet Explorer.

17. Verify that the business contact e-mail is present in the mail_recovery_user inbox.

18. Close all open windows.

EXERCISE 10.6: RECOVERING A MAILBOX STORE USING THE RECOVERY STORAGE GROUP

Estimated completion time: 15 minutes

The first step in recovering mailboxes is to get the relevant mailbox store correctly mounted within the RSG. In this phase of the Contoso Exchange pilot program you will import the mailbox store data you backed up in Exercise 10.3 into the RSG you created in Exercise 10.2.

> **IMPORTANT**   Complete the following tasks on Computerxx and Computeryy.

1. Open Exchange System Manager.

2. Navigate to Administrative Groups, First Administrative Group, Servers, Computerxx (or Computeryy).

3. Right-click Recovery Storage Group, and select Add Database To Recover.

4. In the Select Database To Recover dialog box, select Mailbox Store (Computerxx or Computeryy), and click OK.

5. Review the mailbox store's Properties dialog box, especially the Database tab.

> **NOTE**   When performing this procedure in a production environment, make sure that the location of the RSG has more than enough disk space to hold the entire restored mailbox store.

6. Click OK to close the Mailbox Store (Computerxx or Computeryy) Properties dialog box.

7. Create the folder C:\Restore.

8. From the Start menu, select All Programs, Accessories, System Tools, Backup.

9. On the Backup Or Restore Wizard page, click Advanced Mode Switch From The Wizard Mode.

10. Click the Restore And Manage Media tab. Expand Full_online.bkf, and select the Log Files and Mailbox Store (Computerxx or Computeryy) check boxes as shown in Figure 10-6. Click Start Restore.

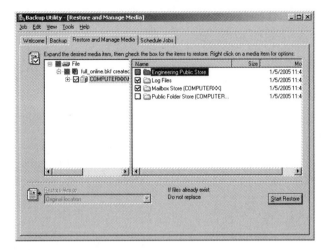

Figure 10-6   Selecting the items to restore

11. In the Restoring Database Store dialog box, enter the temporary location for log and patch files as C:\Restore. Select the Last Restore Set check box, and then click OK.

12. Click Close to close the Restore Progress dialog box. Close the Backup utility.

13. In Exchange System Manager, under the Recovery Storage Group node, right-click Mailbox Store (Computerxx or Computeryy), and select Mount Store.

14. Read the detailed warning message, and then click Yes.

15. Click OK when the mailbox store has been successfully mounted.

EXERCISE 10.7: MERGING RECOVERED MAILBOX DATA

Estimated completion time: 15 minutes

As any administrator knows, one of the most common tasks they will be asked to perform is recovering data that users have accidentally deleted. In this exercise you simulate the accidental deletion of important mailbox data and then recover it from the mailbox store mounted in the RSG.

> **IMPORTANT**   *Complete the following tasks on Computerxx and Computeryy.*

1. If using Computerxx, open OWA by navigating to *http://computerxx/ exchange*. If using Computeryy, open OWA by navigating to *http:// computeryy/exchange*.

2. If using Computer*xx*, log in as e.lang. If using Computer*yy*, log in as c.moon.

3. Delete all items from the Inbox.

4. Close OWA.

5. Open Exchange System Manager.

6. Navigate to Administrative Groups, First Administrative Group, Servers, Computer*xx* (or Computer*yy*), Recovery Storage Group, Mailbox Store (Computer*xx* or Computer*yy*), Mailboxes.

7. If using Computer*xx*, right-click the Eric Lang mailbox, and select Exchange Tasks. If using Computer*yy*, right-click the Christie Moon mailbox, and select Exchange Tasks. This launches the Exchange Tasks Wizard. Click Next.

8. On the Available Tasks page, select Recover Mailbox Data as shown in Figure 10-7. Click Next.

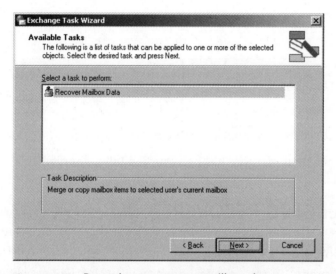

Figure 10-7   Preparing to recover mailbox data

9. On the Recover Mailbox Data page, click Next.

10. On the Recover Mailbox Data page, select Merge Data, and then click Next.

11. Click Next to begin the process immediately.

12. Click Finish to exit the wizard.

13. If using Computer*xx*, open OWA by navigating to *http://computerxx/ exchange*. If using Computer*yy*, open OWA by navigating to *http://computeryy/exchange*.

14. If using Computerxx, log in as e.lang. If using Computeryy, log in as c.moon.

15. Verify that the items that were deleted before from each user's Inbox have been restored.

REVIEW QUESTIONS

Estimated completion time: 20 minutes

1. In your own words, describe what you learned during this lab.

2. What two things are you advised to do when enabling shadow copies on servers that have a high input/output load?

3. You have recently mounted a database in the RSG to restore user mailbox data. You wish to recover data from a different mailbox store. What steps must you take before you can add the new mailbox store for recovery in the RSG?

4. What will happen if you mount a database in the RSG before you restore it from backup?

5. When you restore a user's mailbox data using the Exchange Tasks Wizard, what important components are not restored?

LAB CHALLENGE 10.1: VOLUME SHADOW COPIES AND RESTORING THE EXECUTIVE SG

Estimated completion time: 40 minutes
Part of the pilot program involves assessing the knowledge that you have gained to this point. That includes performing small tasks for which you do not have full instructions, but which you should be able to complete using the knowledge you have gained during today's exercises. You should be able to do the following:

> **IMPORTANT**   *Complete the following tasks on Computerxx and Computeryy.*

■ Create two shadow copy backups. Submit a screen shot showing the original shadow copy backup taken during Exercise 10.2 and the two shadow copy backups taken in the Lab Challenge.

■ Perform a full online backup of the Executive SG storage group.

■ Add the Executive Mailbox Store to the RSG.

■ Perform an online restore of the Executive SG storage group data and log files.

■ Provide a screen shot showing the Executive Mailbox Store successfully mounted in the RSG.

LAB 11
MONITORING MICROSOFT EXCHANGE SERVER 2003

This lab contains the following exercises and activities:

- Exercise 11.1: Filtering Exchange Events in the Application Log

- Exercise 11.2: Monitoring Connected Users

- Exercise 11.3: Monitoring User Mailbox Size

- Exercise 11.4: Configuring Diagnostic Logging

- Exercise 11.5: Specifying Events to Monitor

- Exercise 11.6: Configuring Performance Counters

- Exercise 11.7: Manually Defragmenting a Mailbox Store

- Review Questions

- Lab Challenge 11.1: Logging and Diagnostics

SCENARIO

In this stage of the Contoso Exchange pilot program you will be examining several techniques that your team will need to be familiar with to keep their mail servers healthy. Server health is more than just taking backups. It involves regularly checking logs, monitoring performance, and monitoring user activity. Most serious Microsoft Exchange Server 2003 problems don't just occur out of nowhere. Evidence that these problems are going to occur is likely present in the logs. The aim of this stage of the pilot program is to help train your team to see this evidence when the problems are small, before they become significantly more difficult to manage.

After completing this lab, you will be able to:

- Filter the event log so that you can view only Exchange-specific events.
- Ascertain which users are currently connected to a particular mailbox store.
- Determine the amount of disk space a particular user's mailbox consumes.
- Configure diagnostic logging.
- Configure event monitoring.
- Configure performance counters to monitor server health.
- Perform an offline defragmentation of a mailbox store.

Estimated lesson time: 95 minutes

BEFORE YOU BEGIN

To successfully complete this lab, you will need the following:

- Two networked computers with Microsoft Windows Server 2003 installed using stand-alone configuration according to the setup guide
- Windows Server 2003 CD
- Exchange Server 2003 CD
- To have completed all exercises and lab challenges in Labs 1 through 10

> **IMPORTANT**   This lab is written to be performed on two computers. If each student has only a single computer, students can work as partners and share computers when needed. The first computer will be Computerxx, and the second computer will be Computeryy. Computerxx typically has an odd-numbered name, such as Computer01 and Computer03. Computeryy typically has an even-numbered name, such as Computer02 and Computer04. If you are unsure of your computer's name, run a command prompt and run the hostname command to find out. Unless otherwise specified, all user accounts used in this lab use the password P@ssw0rd.

EXERCISE 11.1: FILTERING EXCHANGE EVENTS IN THE APPLICATION LOG

Estimated completion time: 10 minutes

Log too little, and you are likely to miss something important because it isn't recorded. Log too much, and you are likely to miss something important because although it is recorded, you don't see it because too many other things compete for your attention. Filters allow you to reduce a detailed and broad set of data to a manageable size. To configure filters, follow this procedure.

> **IMPORTANT**   *Complete the following tasks on Computerxx and Computeryy.*

1. Log on with the Administrator account.

2. From the Administrative Tools menu, open Event Viewer.

3. Select the Application Log.

4. From the View menu, select Filter. This opens the Application Properties dialog box.

5. Use the Event Source drop-down list box to select MSExchangeIs Mailbox Store as shown in Figure 11-1.

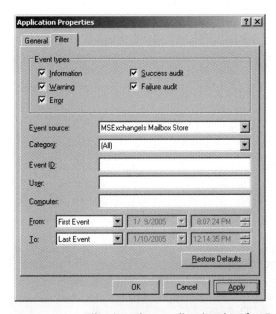

Figure 11-1   Filtering the application log for Exchange events

> **QUESTION**   *What types of events are generated by the MSExchangeIs Mailbox Store event source?*

6. Click OK to apply the filter to the application event log.

7. Close Event Viewer.

EXERCISE 11.2: MONITORING CONNECTED USERS

Estimated completion time: 10 minutes

The easiest way to get a call from an irate user is to shut off a network service that he or she was using in the middle of finishing something important. Before performing maintenance tasks, there is a simple procedure that you can use to determine which users are connected to a particular mailbox or public folder store. This gives you the opportunity to warn users to disconnect before you go about your important maintenance task. To learn how to determine which users are connected to Exchange Server 2003 resources, follow this procedure.

> **IMPORTANT** *Complete the following tasks on Computerxx and Computeryy.*

1. If using Computerxx, open OWA by navigating to *http://computerxx/exchange*. If using Computeryy, open OWA by navigating to *http://computeryy/exchange*.

2. If using Computerxx, log on as s.salavaria. If using Computeryy, log on as c.preston.

3. Minimize Internet Explorer, and open Exchange System Manager.

4. Navigate to Administrative Groups, First Administrative Group, Servers, Computerxx (or Computeryy), First Storage Group, Mailbox Store (Computerxx or Computeryy), and click Mailboxes.

5. Click the header of the Last Logoff Time column to sort accesses by most recent to least recent as shown in Figure 11-2.

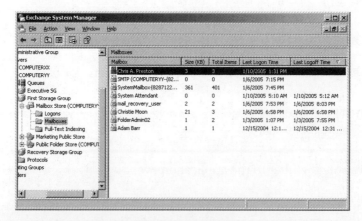

Figure 11-2   Determining last logoff time for user mailboxes

> **QUESTION**   How can you determine which users are still logged on from the information in the Last Logoff Time column of the Mailboxes node of Exchange System Manager?

6. Close all open windows.

EXERCISE 11.3: MONITORING USER MAILBOX SIZE

Estimated completion time: 10 minutes

Something that will be very important once Exchange Server 2003 is deployed throughout Contoso, Ltd. will be how to determine which users are utilizing more than their fair share of disk space. In this phase of the pilot program you will learn how to sort users, from the user who uses the largest amount of storage space to the user who uses the least.

> **IMPORTANT**   Complete the following tasks on Computerxx and Computeryy.

1. Open Exchange System Manager.

2. Navigate to Administrative Groups, First Administrative Group, Servers, Computerxx (or Computeryy), First Storage Group, Mailbox Store (Computerxx or Computeryy), and click Mailboxes.

3. Click the Size (KB) header column to sort mailboxes from largest to smallest.

> **QUESTION**   Why is it that the user with the most items in his or her mailbox might not be the user who consumes the most disk space with his or her mailbox?

4. Close all open windows on both computers.

EXERCISE 11.4: CONFIGURING DIAGNOSTIC LOGGING

Estimated completion time: 10 minutes

Diagnostic logging is useful when you encounter a problem that does not become apparent when looking through the data generated by the normal operation of Exchange Server 2003. Diagnostic logging provides highly detailed information that can shed more light on a problem. The down side to diagnostic logging is that it is only useful over extended periods of time. It generates a massive amount of data that would be impossible to sort through if it was configured to run all the time. To configure diagnostic logging, follow this procedure.

> **IMPORTANT**   *Complete the following tasks on Computerxx and Computeryy.*

1. Open Exchange System Manager.

2. Navigate to Administrative Groups, First Administrative Group, Servers, Computerxx (or Computeryy).

3. Right-click your server, and select Properties.

4. Click the Diagnostics Logging tab.

5. On the Diagnostics Logging tab, under Services, expand MSExchangeIS, and then click Mailbox.

6. Under Category, click General.

7. In the Logging Level box, select Maximum as shown in Figure 11-3.

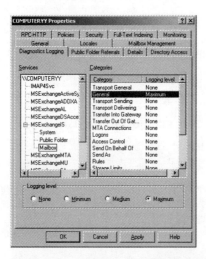

Figure 11-3   Configuring Maximum diagnostic level for mailbox events

8. Click OK to close the Computerxx (or Computeryy) Properties dialog box.

> **QUESTION**   *If your filter from Exercise 11.1 was still applied, would you see more events in the application log when you configure this specific type of diagnostic logging?*

9. Close all open windows on both computers.

EXERCISE 11.5: SPECIFYING EVENTS TO MONITOR

Estimated completion time: 20 minutes

There will be certain events that you want to watch for and certain events that you don't need to know about. Event monitoring allows you to have certain unusual events of interest written to the application log. In this exercise, you learn how to configure event monitoring for Exchange Server 2003.

> **IMPORTANT**   Complete the following tasks on Computerxx and Computeryy.

1. Open Exchange System Manager and navigate to Tools, Monitoring And Status, Status.

2. Double-click Status.

3. View the availability of connectors and servers.

4. Double-click Computerxx (or Computeryy) to open the server object's Properties dialog box.

5. On the Monitoring tab, click Add.

6. In the Add Resource dialog box, click Available Virtual Memory, and then click OK. This opens the Virtual Memory Thresholds dialog box. Set the Duration (Minutes) to **10**, the Warning State (Percent) to **15**, and the Critical State (Percent) to **10** as shown in Figure 11-4. Click OK.

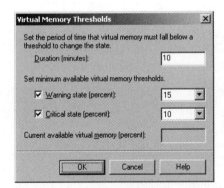

Figure 11-4   Configuring virtual memory monitoring

7. On the Monitoring tab, click Add.

8. In the Add Resource dialog box, select CPU Utilization, and then click OK. This opens the CPU Utilization Thresholds dialog box.

9. In the CPU Utilization Thresholds dialog box, set the Duration (Minutes) to **15**, the Warning State (Percent) to **90**, and the Critical State (Percent) to **95**. Click OK to close the dialog box.

10. On the Monitoring tab, click add.

11. In the Add Resource dialog box, select SMTP Queue Growth.

12. In the SMTP Queue Thresholds dialog box, in the Warning State box, enter **15**, and in the Critical State box, enter **20** minutes. Click OK.

> **QUESTION**   Describe the type of event that would put the SMTP Queue Threshold Monitor into the critical state given the settings in step 12.

13. On the Monitoring tab, click Add.

14. Select Windows 2000 Service, and click OK.

> **IMPORTANT**   Windows 2000 Service also means Windows Server 2003 Services. A forthcoming update to Exchange Server 2003 will rectify this issue.

15. Add both the Microsoft Exchange IMAP4 and Microsoft Exchange POP3 services as shown in Figure 11-5.

Figure 11-5   Configuring virtual memory monitoring

16. Ensure that for each service, the When Service Is Not Running Change State To option is set to Critical.

17. In the Name text box, enter **Mail Servers**, and then click OK.

18. Click Apply.

19. From the Administrative Tools console, open Event Viewer.

20. Select the application log, and check the View menu to ensure that no filtering is currently in use.

21. Minimize Event Viewer.

22. Open the Services console, and stop the Microsoft Exchange POP3 service.

23. Minimize the Services console, and maximize Event Viewer. Click Refresh to update.

> **QUESTION**   What is the source of the three events that appear in the application log after you stop the Microsoft Exchange POP3 service?

24. Maximize the Services console, and restart the Microsoft Exchange POP3 service.

25. Close all open windows.

EXERCISE 11.6: CONFIGURING PERFORMANCE COUNTERS

Estimated completion time: 20 minutes

Performance counters can be used to ascertain how well an Exchange Server 2003 computer is performing under its current load. In the best of worlds, you will have generated a baseline set of figures, so that you know what values are normal and what values are unusual. You can then compare a recent performance log with the baseline to quickly determine which aspects of Exchange Server 2003 performance, if any, have degraded since the server first came online.

> **IMPORTANT**   Complete the following tasks on Computerxx and Computeryy.

1. Log on with the Administrator account.

2. Click Start, select Administrative Tools, and then select Performance.

3. In the console tree, expand Performance Logs And Alerts.

4. Right-click Counter Logs, and then select New Log Settings.

5. In the New Log Settings Name text box, type **MyLog**, and then click OK.

6. On the General tab of the MyLog dialog box, check that the current log file name is the default, C:\PerfLogs\MyLog_000001.blg.

7. Click Add Counters. In the Add Counters dialog box, select Use Local Computer Counters as shown in Figure 11-6.

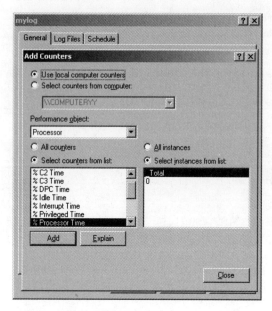

Figure 11-6   Adding performance counters

8. In the Performance Object drop-down list box, select Processor.

9. Select Select Counters From List. In the scroll box below this option, select %Processor Time.

10. Select Select Instances From List, and select _Total. Click Add.

11. Use the same technique to add the following:

   ❑ MSExchangeIS\RPC Requests

   ❑ MSExchangeIS\RPC Operations/sec

   ❑ MSExchangeIS Mailbox\Local delivery rate

   ❑ MSExchangeIS Mailbox\Folder opens/sec

   ❑ MSExchangeIS Mailbox\Message opens/sec

   ❑ PhysicalDisk\Disk Transfers/sec

   ❑ Memory\Pages/sec counter

   ❑ SMTP Server\(_Total)Local Queue Length

   ❑ SMTP Server\(_Total)Messages Delivered/sec counters

12. Click Close.

13. On the General tab of the MyLog dialog box, set the Sample Interval to **5** seconds.

14. Click OK. If you are prompted to create the C:\Perflogs folder, click Yes.

15. In the Performance console, click Counter Logs, and make sure that the MyLog counter log is running. It should be green in color, and if you right-click it, Start should be dimmed.

16. If using Computer*xx*, open OWA by navigating to *http://computerxx/ exchange*. If using Computer*yy*, open OWA by navigating to *http:// computeryy/exchange*.

17. If using Computer*xx*, log on as s.salavaria. If using Computer*yy*, log on as c.preston.

18. Send a new message. If using Computer*xx*, send the message to **c.preston@contosoxx.com**. If using Computer*yy*, send the message to **s.salavaria@contosoxx.com**.

19. In Performance Logs And Alerts, right-click the MyLog log file, and then select Stop.

20. In the console tree, click System Monitor.

21. In the details pane, on the toolbar, click View Log Data.

22. In the System Monitor Properties dialog box, click the Source tab, click Log Files, and then click Add.

23. In the Select Log File dialog box, browse to C:\Perflogs in the Look In box (unless already selected).

24. Click the MyLog_000001.blg log file, and then click Open.

25. In the System Monitor Properties dialog box, click the Data tab, and then click Add.

26. In the Add Counters dialog box, ensure that Use Local Computer Counters is selected. Select each performance object type, all counters, and click Add. When you have added all possible counters, click Close. The Data tab should resemble Figure 11-7.

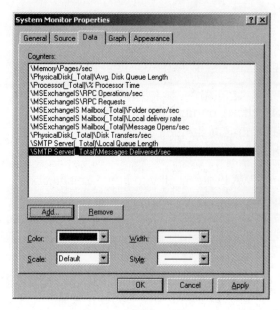

Figure 11-7 System Monitor Properties dialog box

27. Click OK to close the System Monitor Properties dialog box.

28. Use the toolbar to view the data in graph, histogram, and report format. You should be able to locate the moment that you were interacting with OWA.

29. Close all open windows.

EXERCISE 11.7: MANUALLY DEFRAGMENTING A MAILBOX STORE

Estimated completion time: 15 minutes

It is possible that a mailbox store can become so fragmented that the online routines do not significantly improve things. Heavily fragmented stores can cause delays in accessing mail. When a store becomes heavily fragmented, the best option is to perform an offline defragmentation. You'll have to take the store offline, but when the defragmentation is complete, users will notice a significant performance improvement. To perform an offline manual defragmentation, follow this procedure.

> **IMPORTANT** *Complete the following tasks on Computerxx and Computeryy.*

1. Open Exchange System Manager.

2. Navigate to Administrative Groups, First Administrative Group, Servers, Computerxx (or Computeryy), First Storage Group.

3. Right-click Mailbox Store, and select Dismount Store.

4. Review the warning box, and then click Yes to dismount the mailbox store.

5. Open a command prompt, and navigate to the \Program files\Exchsrvr\Bin directory.

6. At the command prompt, type **eseutil /d "c:\program files\exchsrvr\mdbdata\priv1.edb"** and press ENTER.

7. View the output in the command prompt window to verify that the process completed successfully, as shown in Figure 11-8.

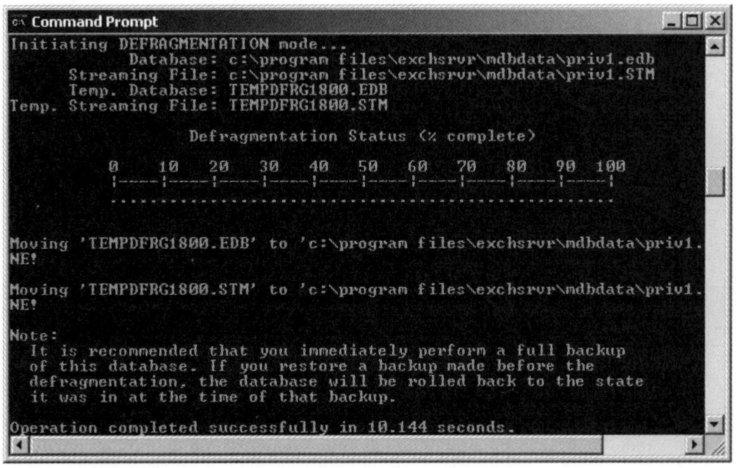

Figure 11-8   Verify that the process completed successfully

8. In Exchange System Manager, right-click Mailbox Store, select Mount Store, and then click OK to acknowledge that the mailbox store was successfully mounted.

REVIEW QUESTIONS

Estimated completion time: 15 minutes

1. In your own words, describe what you learned during this lab.

2. What must you do before using the eseutil utility to perform a defragmentation?

3. What are the three event IDs for the events written to the application log after you configured monitoring and then manually stopped the Microsoft Exchange POP3 service in Exercise 11.5?

4. What is the main consequence of dismounting a mailbox store?

LAB CHALLENGE 11.1: LOGGING AND DIAGNOSTICS

Estimated completion time: 40 minutes

Part of the pilot program involves assessing the knowledge that you have gained to this point. That includes performing small tasks for which you do not have full instructions, but which you should be able to complete using the knowledge you have gained during today's exercises. To finish this assessment, do the following:

> **IMPORTANT**   Complete the following tasks on Computerxx and Computeryy.

■ Create an application log filter that displays only information related to public store events. Submit a screen shot of the filter properties to your instructor.

■ You should only use diagnostic logging when necessary, as it can have a significant impact on server performance. Reduce the diagnostics logging level for the General category of the MSExchangeIS Mailbox event type to None. Submit a screen shot showing this revised setting to your instructor.

■ Perform an offline defragmentation, using the eseutil utility of the public folder store. Provide a screen shot of the command prompt output when the defragmentation is complete. Remember to return the public folder store to its original state when you have completed the defragmentation.

TROUBLESHOOTING MICROSOFT EXCHANGE SERVER 2003

This lab contains the following exercises and activities:

- Exercise 12.1: Using Netdiag to Test Network Connectivity

- Exercise 12.2: Using Dcdiag to Test Domain Controller Connectivity

- Exercise 12.3: Verifying Mailbox Store Integrity

- Exercise 12.4: Configuring a Queue Alert

- Exercise 12.5: Using Telnet to Test the SMTP Server

- Review Questions

- Lab Challenge 12.1: Verifying the Integrity of the Executive Mailbox Store

- Lab Challenge 12.2: Configuring an Alert for IMAP4 Authentication Failures

SCENARIO

The final phase of the Contoso Exchange pilot program is training your team to troubleshoot problems. The first type of problem that they will diagnose is network connectivity. Once network connectivity has been established, team members will diagnose connectivity to domain controllers. Other techniques that will be covered in this final phase include how to verify the integrity of a mailbox store, how to configure a Simple Mail Transfer Protocol (SMTP) queue alert, and how to use telnet to verify that the SMTP server is functioning properly.

After completing this lab, you will be able to:
- **Use netdiag to test network connectivity.**
- **Use dcdiag to test domain controller connectivity.**
- **Verify mailbox store integrity.**

■ Configure an alert to be sent when the SMTP queue reaches a specified size.

■ Use telnet to interact with the SMTP server.

Estimated lesson time: 75 minutes

BEFORE YOU BEGIN

To successfully complete this lab, you will need the following:

■ Two networked computers with Microsoft Windows Server 2003 installed using stand-alone configuration according to the setup guide

■ Windows Server 2003 CD

■ Exchange Server 2003 Enterprise Edition CD

■ To have completed all exercises and Lab Challenges in Labs 1 through 11

> **IMPORTANT**   This lab is written to be performed on two computers. If each student has only a single computer, students can work as partners and share computers when needed. The first computer will be Computerxx and the second computer will be Computeryy. Computerxx typically has an odd-numbered name, such as Computer01 and Computer03. Computeryy typically has an even-numbered name, such as Computer02 and Computer04. If you are unsure of your computer's name, run a command prompt and run the hostname command to find out. Unless otherwise specified, all user accounts used in this lab use the password P@ssw0rd.

EXERCISE 12.1: USING NETDIAG TO TEST NETWORK CONNECTIVITY

Estimated completion time: 10 minutes

Netdiag is a utility included with the Windows Server 2003 support tools. These tools were installed during the very first phase of the Contoso Exchange pilot program, before you installed Exchange Server 2003. To learn how to use netdiag, follow this procedure.

> **IMPORTANT**   Complete the following tasks on Computerxx and Computeryy.

1. Log on with the Administrator account.

2. Open a command prompt.

3. Create the directory C:\Tests

4. Issue the command **netdiag /debug /fix > c:\tests\netdiag1.txt**.

5. When the command completes its execution, issue the command **notepad "c:\tests\netdiag1.txt"**.

6. Review the output, as shown in Figure 12-1.

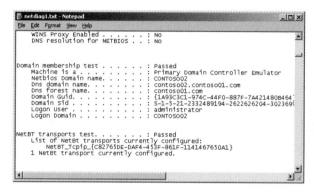

Figure 12-1 Output of netdiag

7. Scroll through and check some of the diagnostic information.

> **QUESTION**   According to the output, what is the first type of configuration information that netdiag /debug /fix attempts to collect?

EXERCISE 12.2: USING DCDIAG TO TEST DOMAIN CONTROLLER CONNECTIVITY

Estimated completion time: 10 minutes

Dcdiag is a diagnostic utility that is used specifically to determine how well the computer on which it runs can communicate with the organization's domain controllers. To learn how to use dcdiag, follow this procedure.

> **IMPORTANT**   Complete the following tasks on Computerxx and Computeryy.

1. Open a command prompt.

2. If using Computerxx, issue the command **dcdiag /s:computerxx / n:contosoxx.com /u: contosoxx\administrator /p:* /v / f:c:\tests\dcdiag1.txt /fix**. If using Computeryy, issue the following command **dcdiag /s:computeryy /n:contosoyy.contosoxx.com /u: contosoyy\administrator /p:* /v / f:c:\tests\dcdiag1.txt /fix**.

3. You will be asked for your password. Enter **P@ssw0rd**.

4. Issue the command **notepad "c:\tests\dcdiag1.txt"**.

5. Review the information located in the Dcdiag1.txt file.

> **QUESTION**   What two connectivity tests are made in the initial required tests?

6. On Computer*xx*, open the Services console and stop the DNS Server service.

7. If using Computer*xx*, issue the command **dcdiag /s:computerxx / n:contosoxx.com /u: contosoxx\administrator /p:* /v / f:c:\tests\dcdiag2.txt /fix**. If using Computer*yy*, issue the command **dcdiag /s:computeryy /n:contosoyy.contosoxx.com /u: contosoyy\administrator /p:* /v /f:c:\tests\dcdiag2.txt /fix**.

8. You will be asked for your password. Enter **P@ssw0rd**.

9. Issue the command **notepad "c:\tests\dcdiag2.txt"**.

10. Review the information located in the Dcdiag2.txt file.

> **QUESTION**   According to the output, what suggestion is made at the end of the initial required tests but before the primary tests?

11. Start the DNS Server service on Computer*xx*.

EXERCISE 12.3: VERIFYING MAILBOX STORE INTEGRITY

Estimated completion time: 20 minutes

Mailbox stores can become corrupted. One indicator of corruption is when the number of messages a user has according to the mailbox store display does not match the number that are actually stored in the user's mailbox. To learn how to verify mailbox store integrity manually, follow this procedure.

> **IMPORTANT**   Complete the following tasks on Computer*xx* and Computer*yy*.

1. Open Exchange System Manager.

2. Navigate to Administrative Groups, First Administrative Group, Servers, Computer*xx* (or Computer*yy*), First Storage Group, Mailbox Store (Computer*xx* or Computer*yy*).

3. Right-click Mailbox Store and select Dismount Store.

4. Review the warning and click Yes.

5. Open a command prompt. Navigate to the \Program files\Exch-srvr\Bin directory.

6. If using Computer*xx*, issue the command **isinteg –s Computer*xx* –test allfoldertests**. If using Computer*yy*, issue the command **isinteg –s Computer*yy* –test allfoldertests**.

7. You are presented with a menu in the command prompt as shown in Figure 12-2.

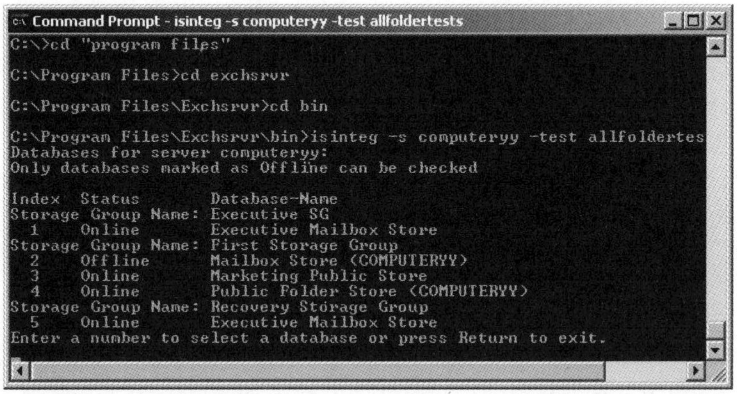

Figure 12-2   The isinteg menu

8. Enter the number that corresponds with Mailbox Store (Computer*xx* or Computer*yy*). It will be the only one that has the status marked as Offline. Press ENTER.

9. You will be asked to verify your selection. Type **Y** and press ENTER.

10. Verify that no errors have occurred.

11. In Exchange System Manager, mount the mailbox store.

> **QUESTION**   Under what condition would you be unable to run isinteg, assuming that you have the appropriate rights?

12. Close all open windows.

EXERCISE 12.4: CONFIGURING A QUEUE ALERT

Estimated completion time: 15 minutes

Queue alerts can immediately notify an administrator if a particular event occurs. You are examining queue alerts as part of the final phase of the Contoso

Exchange pilot program because there are certain Exchange Server 2003 events that your team will need to know about the moment they occur, rather than when they review the logs each morning. To configure these types of alerts, follow this procedure.

> **IMPORTANT**   *Complete the following tasks on Computerxx and Computeryy.*

1. From the Administrative Tools menu, open the Performance console.

2. Expand the Performance Logs And Alerts node, right-click Alerts, and then select New Alert Settings.

3. In the New Alert Settings Name text box, type **SMTP Queue Alert**. Click OK.

4. On the General tab of the SMTP Queue Alert Properties dialog box, type **Alert If Over 30 Messages In Queue**. Click Add. This opens the Add Counters dialog box.

5. In the Performance Object drop-down list box, select MSExchangeIS Mailbox. In the Select Counters from list box, make sure that Send Queue Size is selected. In the Select Instances From list box, select First Storage Group-Mailbox Store (Computerxx or Computeryy). Click Add. Click Close.

6. On the General tab of the SMTP Queue Alert Properties dialog box, ensure that the counter is selected, and then in the Limit text box, type **30** as shown in Figure 12-3.

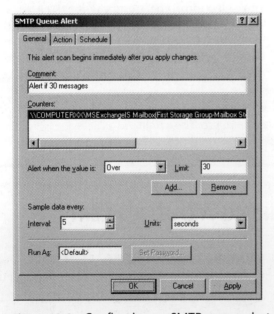

Figure 12-3   Configuring an SMTP queue alert

7. On the Action tab, select Send A Network Message To and type **Administrator** in the associated box. Click OK.

8. In the Performance console, click Alerts. In the details pane, confirm that the alert has started.

> **QUESTION**   How can you ensure that the alert has started?

9. Close all open windows.

EXERCISE 12.5: USING TELNET TO TEST THE SMTP SERVER

Estimated completion time: 20 minutes

Telnet can be used to perform basic diagnostic tasks on an SMTP server, by connecting directly to port 25. Although usually a method of last resort, it is a technique that you want the Contoso Exchange Server 2003 team to be familiar with. To use telnet to test the SMTP server, follow this procedure.

> **IMPORTANT**   Complete the following tasks on Computerxx and Computeryy.

1. Open a command prompt.

2. Issue the command **telnet localhost 25**.

3. You are presented with the Microsoft ESMTP Mail Service header. Enter the command **helo** and press ENTER.

4. Enter the command **mail from:s.salavaria@contoso**xx**.com** and press ENTER.

> **NOTE**   You will receive a message, "Must issue a STARTTLS command first."

5. Type the command **starttls** and press ENTER.

> **QUESTION**   Why is a starttls command required?

6. In Exchange System Manager, edit the properties of your computer's default SMTP virtual server.

7. On the Access Tab, click Communication. Clear the Require Secure Channel check box as shown in Figure 12-4 and click OK.

Figure 12-4 Removing the requirement for encrypted sessions to the SMTP server

8. Click Authentication and select the Anonymous Access check box.

9. Click OK again to close the Default SMTP Virtual Server Properties dialog box.

10. Stop and then start the default SMTP virtual server.

11. At a command prompt, issue the command **telnet localhost 25**.

12. You are presented with the Microsoft ESMTP Mail Service header. Enter the command **helo** and press ENTER.

13. Type the command **mail from:s.salavaria@contosoxx.com** and press ENTER.

> **QUESTION**   What message do you receive when you issue the mail from:s.salavaria@contosoxx.com command this time?

14. If using Computerxx, type the command **rcpt to:s.salavaria@contosoxx.com** and press ENTER. If using Computeryy, type the command **rcpt to:c.preston@contosoxx.com** and press ENTER.

15. Type the command **data** and press ENTER.

16. Type **Subject: Telnet Test E-mail** and press ENTER.

17. Type **This is a test e-mail written using the telnet utility** and press ENTER.

18. Type . and press ENTER.

> **NOTE**   This ends the e-mail and you receive a message saying it is queued for delivery.

19. Enter the command **quit** and press ENTER.

REVIEW QUESTIONS

Estimated completion time: 20 minutes

1. In your own words, describe what you learned during this lab.

2. What message is returned about the IP stack if the IP lookback ping test is passed when the netdiag command was issued in Exercise 12.1?

3. List the five dcdiag primary tests that were omitted by user request.

4. Under what conditions would the alert configured in Exercise 12.4 be triggered?

5. Which SMTP command is used to end an e-mail message?

LAB CHALLENGE 12.1: VERIFYING THE INTEGRITY OF THE EXECUTIVE MAILBOX STORE

Estimated completion time: 20 minutes

Part of the pilot program involves assessing the knowledge that you have gained to this point. That includes performing tasks for which you do not have full instructions, but which you should be able to complete using the knowledge you have gained during today's exercises.

> **IMPORTANT**   *Complete the following task on Computerxx and Computeryy.*

■ Use isiutil to verify the integrity of the Executive Mailbox Store. Provide a screen shot of isiutil's output in the command prompt and submit it to your instructor. Remember to return the Executive Mailbox Store to its original status when you have finished.

LAB CHALLENGE 12.2: CONFIGURING AN ALERT FOR IMAP4 AUTHENTICATION FAILURES

Estimated completion time: 20 minutes

Part of the pilot program involves assessing the knowledge that you have gained to this point. That includes performing tasks for which you do not have full instructions, but which you should be able to complete using the knowledge you have gained during today's exercises.

IMPORTANT   *Complete the following task on Computerxx and Computeryy.*

■ Configure an alert to send a message to the administrator when 10 or more IMAP4 authentication failures occur. Take a screen shot of the General tab of the Alert Properties dialog box and submit it to your instructor.

TROUBLESHOOTING LAB C

RESTORING FROM BACKUP AND PROTOCOL PROBLEMS

Troubleshooting Lab C is a practical application of the knowledge you have acquired from Labs 10, 11, and 12. Your instructor or lab assistant has changed your computer configuration, causing it to "break." Your task in this lab is to apply your acquired skills to troubleshoot and resolve the break. A scenario is presented that will lay out the parameters of the break and the conditions that must be met for the scenario to be resolved. This troubleshooting lab has two break scenarios. The first break scenario involves restoring items deleted from a user's mailbox and the second break scenario involves correcting protocol configuration problems.

> **NOTE**   **Do Not Proceed with This Lab Until You Receive Guidance from Your Instructor**   The break scenario that you will be performing will depend on which computer you are using. The first computer will be Computerxx and the second computer will be Computeryy. Computerxx typically has an odd-numbered name, such as Computer01 and Computer03. Computeryy typically has an even-numbered name, such as Computer02 and Computer04. If you are unsure of your computer's name, run a command prompt and issue the hostname command. If you are using Computerxx, you will perform Break Scenario 1. If you are using Computeryy, you will perform Break Scenario 2. Your instructor or lab assistant might also have special instructions. Consult with your instructor before proceeding.

BREAK SCENARIO 1

> **IMPORTANT**   Perform this break scenario on Computerxx.

This morning, user s.salavaria received a virus that deleted the entire contents of her inbox. You have disinfected her computer and she would like you to restore the lost items. You take a full online backup of all mailbox stores on Computerxx each night. Last night's backup, Thursday.bkf, is located in the C:\Backups directory.

As you resolve the problem, fill out the worksheet in the TroubleshootingLabC folder and include the following information:

- Description of the problem
- A list of all steps taken to diagnose the problem, even the ones that did not work
- Description of the exact issue and solution
- A list of the tools and resources you used to help solve this problem

BREAK SCENARIO 2

IMPORTANT   Perform this break scenario on Computeryy.

Computeryy is having trouble contacting other computers on the network.

As you resolve the problem, fill out the worksheet in the TroubleshootingLabC folder and include the following information:

- Description of the problem
- A list of all steps taken to diagnose the problem, even the ones that did not work
- Description of the exact issue and solution
- A list of the tools and resources you used to help solve this problem